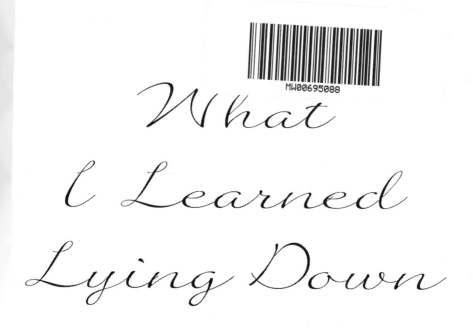

What I Learned Lying Down

HOPE FOR THE CHRONICALLY ILL

Advantage™
INSPIRATIONAL

ANGELA DUGI

In loving memory of my father, James Truman Baker, who courageously fought cancer while teaching me faith and perseverance in the face of death. I look forward, with anticipation, to our heavenly reunion! I love you and miss you Daddy.

Table of Contents

Acknowledgements

To my sweet husband Greg, who patiently encouraged me through waves of doubt and discouragement. Without his constant support and wisdom this book would not have been completed. Thank you for your superb technical support (God knew I was no computer whiz). And for all the times you dropped what you were doing when I asked, "Could you look at a *few* things for me?" (It was never a just a few things, was it?) I know you have a reward in heaven for all the hours you spent helping me edit this book! I love you so much.

To my gifts from God: Mathew, Mary and Emma, you are my life and sweetest joys on earth. God has taught me many lessons through you and I'm still learning! You have been extremely patient with your mom as I worked on this long project, and I've been amazed at your understanding. Your stories, woven throughout, make this book very touching to me and I hope to others as well. Thank you for letting me share. I love you with all my heart. It's finished guys!

To my Mom and friend, Barbara: You have always believed in me and were there for us at a moment's notice. Thank you for placing your life on hold for years, while you served, blessed, prayed and cried with us. From the start, you were enthusiastic about my writing and your confidence in me made such a difference. I'm so grateful for your never-ending encouragement and our frequent phone calls when I needed a listening ear. Mother you are precious, and I love you and Al dearly.

To my wonderful in-laws, Chester and Melba: Thank you for numerous visits to take care of the children while I had doctor appointments, hospital stays or procedures. I cannot begin to count how many loads of laundry you folded or how many times you cleaned out our garage. You kept our household running when we could not. Your unconditional love has been a sweet gift from God and I thank Him for your example.

To my dear friend and prayer warrior, Cindi: Remember those journals you brought me in the early stages of this project as a reminder to keep writing? God really used you to hold me accountable to the call. You are a faithful friend, always reflecting Christ as you encouraged and prayed for me and my family. Without your friendship and fervent prayers, I might have given up. I love you my sister!

To Charles and Beth, our third set of "grandparents" and dearly loved friends: Thank you for your compassion, counsel and listening ears. God knew that we would need you and we praise Him that you adopted us as family. We love you!

To all those who prayed for us throughout the years: My family, precious friends, "email angels" and my brothers and sisters at Global Media Outreach, you will never know this side of heaven how you helped us survive.

To my church family at Champion Fellowship, you are a gift to me. I treasure your hugs, phone calls, prayers and fellowship. Thank you for the meals and for the faithful pick-up crews who delivered my kids home from school daily. You are dearly loved!

To the people of Pecan Grove Baptist, you will always hold a special place in our hearts for how you served and supported us when we were in great need. We will always remember the lawn care, maid service, meals, prayers, visits, babysitting and even packing the moving boxes! Blessings to you all.

To Salem-Sayers Baptist Church: Whenever we were in need of prayer, you were there – praying from afar. Thank for your faithfulness and love for us. To Mildred: You sent me an email three years ago which read, "Write that Book!" The Lord used that email to kick start the whole book writing process. Thank you for encouraging a sister you hardly even knew. I love you.

To Dr. John and Chicki: Thank you for being so gracious in letting us experience "Life on the Farm". It was definitely God's will for us to meet. Bless you for the house calls and helping this difficult patient through the years. We will never forget all you have done for us!

To Bob and Jean: You made "Miracles in New Mexico" possible; it was an adventure that we will never forget. All our love to you dear saints!

To my editor, Patty Norman: Your insight, wonderful suggestions and encouragement were so needed. When I was anxious, you calmed me. Thanks for your patience with this novice writer.

To Jeanne Deimer, Pat Theriault and Mike Janiczek at Advantage Books, I deeply appreciate how you shared my vision for this book and believed in me.

Thank you, precious Holy Spirit, for being my inspiration. You gave me just what I needed each time I wrote. Father, I love you and praise your name for allowing me to do this work to glorify you. Jesus, you are my Everything! Thank you for your tender love for me.

To my sweet Aunts, cousins, friends and all who endure the pain of chronic illness: This book is written with you in mind.

Foreword

by Greg Dugi

Fifteen years ago, as Angie and I said "I do", we could have no idea the journey we were about to embark on together. Of course, we had all the typical emotions of newlyweds; being deeply in love and having hopes for a wonderful life together. No couple expects tragedy or looks for trouble as they begin their life together as husband and wife.

I had remained single up through the age of thirty, wondering if I would every find "Mrs. Right," yet here she was standing before me in white. I knew deep in my soul that she was "the one" (I had known it from our second date).

While it took a long time to work up the courage to actually ask her to marry me, here we finally were, standing in front of God, friends and family to make a life-long commitment. We took our vows very seriously. I remember being so excited and yet so deeply worried on our wedding way – worried that I might fail at this marriage thing. The last thing I ever wanted to do was fail God or my new wife.

As vows were recited, I felt a tingling chill as I repeated each one aloud, realizing the gravity of what I was saying. For some reason, the words "in sickness and in health" came easy. After all, we were fairly young and healthy; it just didn't seem as serious as the other commitments.

Eventually, all marriages are tested, sometimes severely, some frequently and some endlessly. It was at the time our second child was born, that our true test began. Over the ten plus years that followed, God would allow our world to be turned upside down. Our faith was shaken to its core; our love for each other was wrung out until it was nearly dried up; and our hopes for the simple pleasures of life and growing old together were smashed.

Through this trial, I failed my wife, my family and my God many times. But today, as you read this book, I say with all surety, "God's grace has carried us through." The vicious disease that tried to wreck our marriage, family and my career has failed to do so. Our faith in the Lord is stronger than ever and our love for each other is deeper than I could have imagined. Our three children have learned what is important in life and how to serve others; they are only loosely attached to the things of this material life and each has a strong faith in Christ.

We have witnessed first-hand just what Jesus meant when He said, "I will never leave you nor forsake you."

Angie started writing about her experience with a mysterious and chronic illness by keeping a journal. Recording her thoughts and feelings was a way to cope. A few years ago, she clearly heard a voice in her spirit that told her to start writing something bigger than a journal. What you now hold in your hands is a result of her obedience to that call.

I will admit that at first, I didn't know what to think about this new project of hers. Life was so impossible at that time and our relationship was often adversarial. I was already feeling resentment at how the disease had kidnapped my wife from me—there was so little "normal" time. Now in addition to her mind being distracted by pain, there was a new focus—another one that didn't include me. We were in two different worlds. To her, this book was a reason for pressing on and a chance to turn pain into blessing. For me, it was yet another way to lose her.

The project has been long and as any author can tell you, it has consumed much of her time and energies. Nevertheless, I have been blessed as I watched the passion and drive of a woman (often racked with pain and fatigue or worse) determined to tell her story.

Her purpose has been simple: to provide hope and support to the chronically ill and to those that love and care for them. She desires to identify with those who suffer quietly while the world marches on; suffering not only in the body, but also as the trauma of serious illness attempts to tear down their relationships, their faith and eventually, their spirit.

"What I Learned Lying Down" is her story and it is also our story. It is a story not of physical healing but of spiritual growth and healing of the soul. I hope that as you read, you will both laugh and cry, feeling the love poured out from her heart to yours, as she tells of the power of God to change pain into joy and trauma into peace. May God lead you into new places of hope and peace as you read Angie's story.

Introduction
by Angela Dugi

On March 15, 2004, I was awakened at 2:00 a.m., by the Lord's familiar voice saying, *"I want you to start writing...and I want you to write the end of your story first...how I healed you."* His voice was clear and unmistakable and at that moment I knew what God was calling me to do. This book is written in obedience to Him so I might share what I learned through many quiet hours, when illness forced me to lie down.

This is a personal story of my battle with an often disabling illness that has radically changed everything about my life, my marriage, my parenting and even my faith. With an unwavering desire to hold on to God, no matter what, He has brought me and my family through turbulent trials that have taken us to the very edge and back again. My prayer is that this story will bring hope, comfort and encouragement to those who suffer with chronic illness and disease, as well as to those who care for them.

As you read the pages that follow, I pray you gain strength from the lessons that God taught me through His Word, and the experiences recounted in this book. You may even find yourself laughing a little along the way. For those of you who are suffering, I hope you will be able to identify with my struggles and find that you are not alone.

This book has been written from the position of the afflicted one - me. The entire time that it was being penned, I struggled with multiple health problems. Perhaps writing through the pain has served to paint an even more candid picture of what life is truly like living with chronic illness.

If you are plagued with an unrelenting disease, or maybe you have a loved one who is seriously ill, consider this book to be a heartfelt hug from me to you!

God rarely does things the way we expect Him to. He is God, we are not. His hand stretched out the heavens, calling out the stars by name. Even the lightning bolts report to Him and the wind and the waves obey Him! He spoke the earth into existence and His power is far beyond our limited minds. He never grows tired or weary and His understanding no one can fathom. The Lord's ways are beyond measure as described in the following verse:

For my thoughts are not your thoughts, neither are your ways my ways, declares the LORD. As the heavens are higher than the earth, so are my ways higher than your ways and my thoughts than your thoughts. (Isaiah 55:8-9)

Almost twelve years have passed since the onset of my illness, yet I am still afflicted. I have fasted, prayed, waited and believed for a miraculous healing; however the illness remains. I have been anointed with oil seven times, and been prayed for by literally hundreds of people. I've even surrendered my longing to be healed to the Lord, thinking that surely this must be what He is waiting for. But God was not waiting on me. Friends, no stone has been left unturned. But here I sit, content, writing and accepting where I am today by the grace of God.

May I suggest to you that a miracle *has* taken place? The miracle I propose is that of God's grace to sustain the sick, day after day, knowing that they may have to live the rest of their lives fighting for their health. It is God's sovereign will that directs our paths. Some of His children are healed on earth, and others He takes home for the ultimate healing.

Praise God...The Lord has healed my heart, mind and emotions, and one day in heaven I will be completely whole, trading in this lowly body, for one like my Savior's glorious one!

Our citizenship is in heaven, and we eagerly await a Savior from there, the Lord Jesus Christ, who, by the power that enables him to bring everything under his control, will transform our lowly bodies so that they will be like His glorious body. (Philippians 3:20-21)

I Needed The Quiet

I needed the quiet so He drew me aside.
Into the shadows where we could confide.
Away from the bustle where all the day long
I hurried and worried when active and strong.
I needed the quiet tho at first I rebelled
But gently, so gently, my cross He upheld
And whispered so sweetly of spiritual things
Tho weakened in body, my spirit took wings
To heights never dreamed of when active all day.
He loved me so greatly He drew me away.
I needed the quiet, No prison my bed,
But a beautiful valley of blessing instead.
A place to grow richer in Jesus to hide.
I needed the quiet so He drew me aside.

-Alice Hansche Mortenson

Chapter 1

Before the Storm

Lying down is the perfect position for sleeping, but when a chronic illness and its constant fatigue force you down, that is altogether different. Sometimes the Lord makes us lie down; leading us beside still waters, restoring our souls (Psalm 23). Due to the nature of my affliction, I have been given a great deal of practice at being still. This has been often difficult, however the end result has been priceless treasures that the Lord has taught me while lying down.

Before I go on, let me briefly tell you about my life before illness.

I am the oldest of three children, having grown up in a loving and nurturing home where my mother and father raised me, my younger sister and brother. My parents loved each other deeply, and there was never a question of their love for us.

I have many childhood memories that I cherish. Some of my fondest memories are of family vacations, camping out or going to the beach. We were also very close to our extended family and enjoyed spending time with relatives. All my needs were provided for and much more. Life was good, but just like any other family we had our trials as well.

Both of my parents loved to cook, but my Mom was especially strict about teaching us healthy eating habits. I think we may have been one of the first families that tossed the white bread for wheat, whole milk for skim, and fried chicken for Shake N' Bake. Captain Crunch cereal was something my siblings and I eyed on the grocery shelf, but somehow it never made it into Mom's basket. None of those yummy presweetened cereals for us! However, having three kids of my own, I now appreciate her resolve to feed us nutritiously.

Mother faithfully took us to Sunday school and church, and I watched as she read her Bible every night before she went to sleep. I am eternally grateful for her example and the lasting impact it made on me, and in turn, my children. Eventually, my dad gave his life to Christ, and it was a wonderful moment for us all. Over the years, I had the pleasure of watching him grow in the Lord, reading and studying the Word.

At the age of ten years old, I asked Jesus to be Lord of my life. I vividly remember the nudging of the Holy Spirit calling me to follow Him. It was the most important decision I have ever made. Joy filled me as my walk with the Lord began, and I could not wait to tell all my fourth grade friends about this Jesus who now lived in me (only they weren't quite as excited as I was).

During my teen years I was active and involved in several school activities. I was a good student, finding my niche in playing the flute, and eventually graduated in the top ten percent of my class. After graduation I was offered a position as a dental assistant, developing a new hobby – teeth. Because of this job, I felt that God was leading me into dentistry, so I decided to apply at a dental hygiene school (I wanted a profession that required as little math as possible, and this was one of the perks). The dental field was fascinating to me, and in time I earned a degree in Applied Science. Unfortunately, as

I excelled in my studies and potential career, I left God behind.

On weekends, I attended parties with the other students and began drinking. As I drifted farther away from the Lord, I could no longer hear His voice. Consequently, I made choices that were out of God's will for my life. This led to an abusive relationship that ended in abandonment, and sadly, divorce. I felt rejected and completely devastated.

At one point, I wanted to end my life by driving off a very high bridge, and it was then the Lord reminded me of Philippians 4:13: *"I can do everything through him who gives me strength."* That verse gave me hope that I urgently needed to press on. I could carry on, not in my strength, but His alone! I cried out to the Lord for help, asking him to heal my broken heart, and over time, He did just that. I asked for God's forgiveness and rededicated my life to Him when I was 23 years old, discovering that we serve a God of second chances and new beginnings.

From that moment on, I buried myself in my Bible, prayer and Christian music. I wanted to make up for precious time lost between me and the Lord. A strong passion and zeal for the Lord consumed me like never before, which gave me unspeakable joy! I look back on this beloved time and realize this is when Jesus became my best friend.

I was attending a large church in the Houston area during this time. I was content being single and had no desire to remarry whatsoever. Little did I know, I was about to meet the godly man that I have been married to for the past 15 years.

I met Greg while he was teaching a singles' Sunday school class. Initially, I was drawn to him because of his knowledge of the Bible, but I also found him handsome and funny. We began dating, and God was in charge this time, not

Angie. We covered our relationship in prayer and after only one month of dating, the Lord assured me that he was "the one."

Greg is an only child and his family came from a relatively fundamentalist church. I expected that my previous marriage and divorce would make it highly unlikely that his parents would accept me for their only son. To my surprise, they welcomed me with open arms, describing Greg as their *Isaac* and me as their *Rebecca*. I was humbled by their display of love and acceptance. I fell in love with their Isaac, and it took us just a few short months to figure out that God's hand of blessing was on our relationship. After one year of dating, we married in the church where we met, and it was a simple, but beautiful wedding. We felt the Spirit of the Lord that day in our midst, and His favor was evident.

Our marriage was harmonious from the beginning. Greg was slow to anger and patient, as well as kind and gentle. These qualities reminded me a lot of my Dad. We both had rewarding careers, and were blessed financially. It seemed we had it all, a beautiful home, new cars, a wonderful family and church home. Both of us were in good health and it seemed like God was smiling down on us. We enjoyed taking long walks together, rollerblading and traveling. I loved aerobics, cooking, shopping, and eating out was a mutual pastime of ours. We both remember thinking, "This must be what living that abundant life is all about." I believed that since I had gone through such a difficult trial early in my life, that the rest of my life would be smooth sailing. Boy, was I naïve! I had no clue as to how much God would teach me and my husband in the years to come.

After just one year of marriage, I desperately wanted to start a family. Greg, being an only child, was not as anxious. I wanted somewhere between four and six children. He wanted one or less. After finding out that nagging him about the issue was not effective, I shut up and prayed, asking God to give him the desire for a child as well. It didn't take long for the Lord to answer that prayer. I was pregnant within a few months, and God granted me the desire of my heart, a precious son.

Matthew was born a "blue baby" which meant he was not getting enough oxygen to his brain. He was four weeks early, and when he did not make a sound at delivery, we feared our baby was dead. He was assigned an extremely low Apgar score (this being the measure of an infant's viability at the moment of birth); however, after a short while on oxygen, he recovered, and we breathed a giant sigh of relief. Of course he was the most beautiful baby we had ever seen, a perfect six pound bundle of pure joy! In his first few weeks, Matthew had a tough bout with jaundice; but after that passed, we found that he was an easy baby, and I felt my life was complete. It was an amazing time, and I loved almost every minute of it. My relationship with the Lord continued to grow, and I often read my Bible while nursing. It was a cherished time of God feeding me while I fed my son.

When Matthew was just nine months old, we found out that I was pregnant again. We were excited, but shocked as gift number two was on its way, and what a timely gift that would be.

What I Learned Lying Down

Chapter 2

Daddy's Dying

...The LORD gave and the LORD has taken away;
may the name of the LORD be praised. (Job 1:21)

What a delightful Thanksgiving surprise! My heart was so full in November of 1996, as I busily decorated our new home. I adored our new son, and now God was blessing us with another gift. I had always looked forward with anticipation to the day that God would make me a mother, and now He was allowing me that honor a second time— it all seemed too good to be true. My delight turned quickly to dismay, however, when I received a phone call that no one is ever prepared for.

It was my mother and she had terrible news. She was calling from the hospital where Dad had been waiting for test results concerning his sudden difficulty breathing. "It's cancer," she said calmly. I knew she must have been in shock because of the calmness in her voice, so I tried to hold myself together while on the phone. After hanging up, I fell apart, weeping uncontrollably. My husband's parents just happened to be visiting us, and they were there to catch me that day and be the strength I did not have. I'll never forget that cold day when my world came crashing down. My mind could not process why God would bless me with this new life at a time when my dad was fighting for his. It was something I would wrestle with the entire pregnancy. God was teaching me about fully trusting in Him.

The first verse I learned in Sunday school was Proverbs 3:5-6. *"Trust in the LORD with all your heart and lean not on your own understanding; in all your ways acknowledge him, and he will make your paths straight."* We would certainly need the Lord to direct this unknown path that lay ahead.

That evening we drove to go see my father in the hospital a few hours away. I cried all the way. My little guy in the back seat thought Mommy was laughing, and would giggle every time I exploded into tears (he had never heard me cry like this before). As we neared the hospital, a feeling of dread engulfed me. We rushed down the hall to his hospital room to wait for the doctor's final report. To add to our grief, we were told he had inoperable lung cancer. These words paralyzed us.

For treatment, they would hit him hard with aggressive chemotherapy, but the doctor gave him only three months to live. As I walked into the hospital room, I stared in disbelief at my dad who had always been a picture of health. He was faithful to get a physical every year, so naturally we wondered how this could have happened.

"Surely there is some way you can remove the tumor?" we pleaded. The doctor then explained that the cancer had metastasized, involving the pleural lining, and for that reason it would be impossible to operate.

What an awful word, "inoperable," I thought.

I'm so thankful that we are not "inoperable" in God's eyes. It doesn't matter how badly we are broken by our sins, we are never beyond repair.

After the terrible news, Dad wanted to leave the hospital immediately, so he discharged himself, and we drove to my parent's home in the country.

I have a precious memory of walking barefoot with my dad around the circular driveway in front of their home that very evening. We were still in a state of shock. My hand was tucked inside my dad's as we walked, occasionally wincing as my tender feet met the hard gravel. Nonetheless, I wouldn't have traded this moment with him for anything in the world. We talked, tearfully sharing encouragement from Romans 8:28. Somehow, this trial would be for our collective good, not just Dad's. God would use this to grow me, as I was about to begin a journey that would give me a whole new perspective on what was truly important in life.

I became painfully aware of how material things had consumed me. Just days before the diagnosis I was unhappy and discontent with the emptiness of our large new home. So much time was spent thinking about how we would furnish and decorate it. Now my father's life was in danger, and I was suddenly ashamed of how out of balance my priorities had become. I chided myself because that all seemed so trivial now. I just wanted Dad to live, period.

Lying in bed, in the darkness of that night, I was distraught over what lay ahead for my precious mom and dad. For the first time in my life, I believe the Holy Spirit graciously gave me a vision. I saw the Lord's hand, and in His large palm was my father's hospital bed where he and Mom were lying peacefully. The comfort this gave me was incredible, and then I was able to fall asleep. What a picture of how God holds each of us in His almighty hand! God was using this crisis to get my focus off the material things that had ensnared me.

A few days later, my mind shifted its focus to the little one growing inside me. At about four months into the pregnancy, I began to bleed and was subsequently put on bed rest. I tried very hard to keep this from Mom (who had enough to deal with), but to no avail, because mothers just have a way of knowing things. The next week my doctor ordered an ultrasound and told me I might have been carrying twins. He saw an empty, ruptured sac, but the other tiny baby was just fine. For a brief time, it saddened me, but in light of everything that was going on, I was very thankful for the life that remained.

We soon found out we would be having a girl. I was so grateful for ultrasound because I wanted to tell Daddy as much about this baby as I could. We had already picked out the name Mary Kate, and it was the sweetest thing for my dad to call and ask, "How is Mary Kate doing today?" He did this frequently, and it gave him some connection to his unborn granddaughter.

As my belly grew, Dad's health declined rapidly. We were now spending a lot of time at M.D. Anderson Cancer Center in Houston. He was hospitalized for three weeks while they hit him hard with powerful drugs that took him within inches of his life. They determined that the cancer was actually melanoma that had metastasized to the lungs, and the devastating news was that it was in stage four. He was so brave and courageous as they tapped his pleural cavity every few days to remove fluid from his lungs. Although he endured much pain, he came alive for Christ! He would boldly tell complete strangers about Jesus who lived in him, and he witnessed to people with such gentleness. I learned so much about life while watching him die. He inspired and challenged me.

Looking back, I am glad he had my pregnancy as a distraction. Dad wanted to help in preparing the baby's room for her arrival, but he was too weak from the chemotherapy.

He did a special thing that brings tears to my eyes even as I write. Unable to stand, lying flat on his back, Daddy instructed my husband how to put a chair rail on the wall of our baby's room. He carefully talked Greg through exactly how to cut and place the wood and it turned out beautifully. My husband could not have done it without my father's engineering talents.

Ironically, as Dad became preoccupied with this little baby growing inside me, I watched as his faith grew within him.

"The Lord woke me up with cancer, and it's the best thing that has ever happened to me," he would say. What a statement from a man who was dying of terminal cancer! That is what my father would say to anyone who would listen, and he had a way about him, with his bright smile and gentle spirit. He would embarrass my mother a little by going up to complete strangers in restaurants and hospitals telling them how good God had been to him, with a tumor bulging out of his back. He wouldn't let people get away very easily—he kind of cornered them. It seems a little funny to me now, but God was using him in a powerful way.

My father had been a believer from the time I was fourteen years old, but as years passed, he drifted away from God. When the doctor told him he had only three months to live, his life changed dramatically. I saw things in my Dad that I had never seen before. He grew so close to the Lord during this short time. The gift of evangelism sprang forth into his life, and I wanted to have his attitude if I ever got sick. He was pleasing the Lord, and my father had joy only Jesus could give.

Our father-daughter relationship was closer than ever, and I could not imagine living without him. For the first time, we would share our favorite scriptures and pray together.

He joined the Texas Baptist Men after the cancer diagnosis, and even in his weakened condition, he helped to build a new church. I was amazed at his determination to work for the Lord with the time he had left. He became my hero and I was extremely proud of him.

If only we lived each day as if it were our last, we would be empowered to do so much for our Lord. Missed opportunities and procrastination would be things of the past. Anyone who crossed our path would be told about the gift of salvation through Jesus Christ. We would let go of grudges, love one another, study God's Word and pray without ceasing. Just eight weeks before the Lord took Daddy home; he was given the opportunity to tell many of what God had done for him.

His pastor asked if he would give his testimony in front of their church. My father jumped at this chance even though he hated to speak in public. By that time, he was very frail and thin. Listening to his testimony was a reminder of II Corinthians 12:10, "...for when I am weak, then I am strong." He spoke to the congregation of how God blessed him with cancer and how his life was now richer than ever! He gave glory to God, and I know many were touched as the church service was televised over several counties. My father certainly left a legacy for his children and grandchildren.

As the tumor began to grow rapidly in his lung, he had increased trouble breathing. It was agonizing to watch the strong one who raised me, slowly waste away. It was dreadful to see and feel the large tumor, now bigger than a baseball, jutting out of his tender back. I was having much trouble understanding why the Lord was letting him suffer in this way. This nearly became a crisis of faith for me and ultimately led to a turning point in my Christian life. Could I really trust this

God whom I loved? Why would God let my dad, who dearly loved Him, suffer so much? The Lord gave me my answer:

Now if we are children, then we are heirs–heirs of God and co-heirs with Christ, if indeed we share in his sufferings in order that we may also share in His glory. (Romans 8:17)

If we want to share in His glory we will suffer in this life. It is when we suffer for Jesus that we can really shine for Him. If we let God have His way in us, our affliction can be a powerful platform through which we can be used. That platform can then give us purpose as we use it for the glory of God.

When I was about eight months pregnant, Daddy's belly began to swell and he looked pregnant like me. I think we both knew he would not get to hold my baby. My strong father, who for thirty-three years took care of Mom, now had to lean on her for everything. Watching Mom lose her best friend was heart wrenching. These were desperate times for us as a family. My sweet dad would say over and over that he could not leave us. He fought terribly to hang on for his family, and he tried to be "Superman" on a few occasions.

I remember one particular day he got a burst of energy and decided to mow the lawn wearing his pajamas. We could tell there would be no stopping him. He got on his riding lawn mower, zooming back and forth with his navy blue bathrobe flying in the wind! We had never seen him do figure eights with the lawn mower, and so we stood back, watching from an inside window where it was safe, smiling as he cut the grass like never before. Because we had cried so much, I think the

Lord knew we needed to laugh. I now know that Dad just needed to *do* something.

Two days before my father died, my husband and I went to visit him one final time. He looked deathly ill and was struggling for every breath. Somehow I knew this was the last day I would see him alive. Before leaving, I went into my parents' bathroom and tried to settle myself. I knelt down and cried out to God asking, "How do I say goodbye?" At that moment, the Holy Spirit spoke clearly to my heart, "*It's only a temporary goodbye.*" I felt the Lord's gentle presence and comfort as I wiped my tears and splashed cold water on my face. Making my way to his recliner, I kissed his sweet forehead for the last time and whispered, "Jesus has not left you...I love you, Daddy." Tears welled up in his eyes and mine, and when I walked out the front door of their house, it felt like I was being ripped in two.

It was one of the hardest moments of my life, leaving him lying in that recliner, knowing that soon I would be driving back to a house where he would no longer live. I remember getting home and dropping to my knees that night, pleading with God to take him home so his suffering would end. Two days later on August 5, 1997, at the age of 54, Dad took his last breath here on earth and saw his first glimpse of his heavenly home.

My family was so relieved that he was no longer suffering, although it broke our hearts that he would not see my baby girl. It was simply beyond my human understanding, yet somehow, I had to trust that God's timing was perfect and that He had not made a mistake.

Returning to my parents' home for the funeral was surreal. The recliner was empty and Daddy wasn't waiting with a hug at the door to greet us as he always had. His glasses, his watch, and even his pens and pencils that were always in his front pocket, were lying there on his night stand. Just seeing his shoes in the closet brought a wave of shock and grief. And then there was the house itself, a vivid reminder of him, given that he had built it with his own hands. I wasn't prepared for the emotions that welled up inside of me, seeing all his personal belongings left behind. It absolutely stunned me!

The apostle Paul writes, *"What is your life? You are a mist that appears for a while and then vanishes"* (James 4:14). We take absolutely nothing with us, only our souls to the eternal destination chosen by us. The treasures we collect, the toys we accumulate, the jewelry, clothes, cars and houses all stay behind. Our bodies are just temporary tents. They will one day die and fade away, but praise Jesus—the Bible says that if we follow Christ we are given a new glorified body in heaven! What a comfort to know that Dad's soul was secure. He was safely home!

What I Learned Lying Down

Chapter 3

Falling Apart

He is before all things, and in him all things hold together. (Colossians 1:17)

On August 28th, just 3 weeks after my dad died, I was talking to my grieving mother on the phone about how much we already missed him. She said, "Angie, I'm ready to hold that little baby." Well, God acted immediately on her request and things started to happen. I was also full-term and ready to deliver this child yesterday! Thank God we had no idea of the dangers that lay ahead.

After hanging up the phone I began to feel very strange. Dizziness set in and I had a throbbing headache and an unusual change in my vision. I hurriedly walked to the bathroom mirror and was frightened to discover that I could not see my right eye in the reflection! Alarmed, I knew that something was very wrong. My in-laws had just come for a visit and were in the kitchen. When I told Greg about my vision loss, his Dad said it was probably just a "floater." I knew this was no floater. I could not see out of one eye! Greg decided to take my blood pressure, and it was through the roof.

My systolic pressure was way out of range so he immediately phoned the doctor on call. We were instructed to get to the hospital as quickly as possible, so we threw our bags in the car and kissed our toddler good-bye. I was so glad that Greg's parents decided to come that day (I believe God arranges these things that we call coincidence). I was nervous on the way to the hospital and had a feeling I would be having this baby soon. Upon arrival, things happened quickly.

The team at the hospital diagnosed acute preeclampsia. My blood pressure was dangerously high (at stroke level) and my vision was still poor. I was at risk for a seizure so they administered anti-seizure medication through an I.V. The nurse told me to rest. I thought to myself, "Umm...I can't see out of my right eye and you just told me you were giving me medication so I wouldn't have a seizure?" I was also not allowed to talk because it raised my blood pressure too much, so I quietly asked Greg to call Mother, and she was quickly on her way.

Tests revealed that I was spilling proteins and my blood-clotting factor was too low. In hind sight, I'm glad that I did not know how dangerous this was. Preeclampsia is a life-threatening disorder where both mom and baby are in danger. I could have easily died or gone into a coma, but God preserved my life and the life of our baby.

The Lord goes before us in all circumstances! In Him all things hold together; He moves the mountain; He calms the storm. He parts the sea so we can cross on dry ground, and without a doubt, He carried me through this scary and painful delivery. It reminds me of one of my favorite verses that we have framed on our living room wall, *"With man this is impossible, but with God all things are possible"* (Matthew 19:26).

When my doctor arrived the next morning, he was upset over not being notified of my severe condition during the night. He decided to induce labor immediately. My very calm doctor, who had actually sung to me during my first delivery, looked worried and anxious. With contractions came even higher blood pressure. We all knew I would not be able to push for very long. Due to the low platelets, a C-section was out of the question because of the risk of hemorrhaging. We were in a dangerous dilemma. The doctor was candid with Greg, telling him that he did not know how we were going to deliver. With God's help would be the only way…that we knew.

I was unable to have an epidural until I was dilated 9 centimeters and in excruciating pain. Greg was on one side of me while my grief-weary mom was on the other. I needed both of them, and they were great support, though terrified (I found out after the delivery that my Mom had just seen an episode of the television show "E.R" where the mother had preeclampsia and died during delivery). The next set of blood tests revealed that finally, by the grace of God, the clotting factor was increasing. Unfortunately, there was yet another problem.

My baby was struggling too. Her arm was over her head and her heart rate was dropping fast. At this point, I actually thought I would not live to see my baby. My blood pressure was nearing 200 and my doctor wasted no time in getting out the forceps. He cut me severely and pulled our baby girl out to safety. She came into this world screaming as my husband and I cried in relief, thanking God for rescuing us. I experienced a miracle that day, and I would never be the same.

Mary Kate was a healthy, beautiful baby girl weighing 7 lb. 12 oz. She was perfect and had my dad's blue eyes. We were so proud of her. On the other hand, I was far from perfect. I was hospitalized for a week with an epidural morphine pump for pain (I'm wishing I had one of those right about now, given that my pain is strong as I write). You just push the little red button and within minutes, voila! No pain. I thought it was the greatest invention ever! I continued to need the I.V. medication because my blood pressure was still elevated, and I was swollen from head to toe.

I am so glad that God is in the repair business because I needed His healing hand in many ways. Holding this precious baby girl helped my mom and I heal from the pain of my father's death. She smiled at only two weeks old, and it was as if God was smiling through her to comfort our sad hearts. I was amazed with God's love and goodness after all those months of asking Him, "Why am I pregnant at this time?" Now I could see so clearly what God knew all along. I finally understood that it was God's mercy in planning her arrival.

We can trust our Father in heaven with those things we don't understand. He knows best. During the pregnancy, I could not see that this baby would be a special healing tool sent from God to help us through our time of grief. In fact, many late nights as I rocked my baby, I felt like God was rocking me. This experience led me to a whole new level of trust in the Lord. That trust is what would see me through the rocky terrain that lay ahead.

When my baby was six weeks old, post-partum depression hit hard. I had struggled with depression before but this was much more intense. I was also adjusting to having two babies eighteen months apart, both in diapers. Grief combined with dropping hormones and a colicky baby was a toxic combination. I was falling apart at the seams. It was at this time we went to see my father's gravesite. I was not at all prepared for the flood of emotion that swept over me as we walked up to the gravestone. I found no comfort at the grave, but was relieved in knowing that Dad's spirit was in heaven— not dead but alive!

Not long after the funeral, my mom and I joined a grief support group at church. It was necessary for us to press on, and since I was nursing baby Mary, she was the youngest attendee. Not only was I was grieving over my loss, but my children's loss, as well. They would not know how wonderful their grandfather was, and how much he loved them. I think I cried every night for a year. In addition, I sensed an enormous responsibility to take care of my mother. I even thought for a time, I could fill in the gap somehow that Dad left behind.

When my daughter was about four months old, I began to develop acute abdominal pains that caused me to double over. With these painful episodes it was difficult to breathe, much less speak. It got so severe that we ended up in the emergency room more than once. I had no idea what was happening, and fear would seize me.

A gastroenterologist ordered scans, X-rays and other tests (you can imagine what was going through our minds after what my father had gone through). I was relieved when test results showed that it was the gallbladder that was likely to be the source of pain. Surgery was recommended, and we agreed to it believing that it would end my pain, but only a short time after the operation the pain came back worse than ever. I was crushed when I realized that an organ had been removed unnecessarily.

Not by our choice, we once again found ourselves in the E.R, running back to the doctors for an answer. Day-to-day life became so difficult that my mother had to practically move in to help us take care of the two little ones.

After more procedures and painful episodes, a specialist told me that I needed to look into pain management. He informed me that there was nothing more that could be done and that I would have to live with this pain for the rest of my life. All I wanted was to be well again, to return to the old me. Greg and I were desperate for help.

Following much prayer the Lord led us to a wise physician who over time has become a dear friend. We were amazed that he did not prescribe any medications or do any procedures. In addition, nothing about my story surprised him; he acted like he had heard it many times before.

Treatment began by changing my diet, adding supplements and teaching me about nutrition. For about six months I fared pretty well, however when the situation began to regress, the doctor found it necessary to add a few medications to keep my gut from wrenching. He explained that I had a motility disorder that affected my entire gastric tract, not just my gallbladder. This explained why the surgery did not help.

Gradually, fatigue moved in and physical weakness at times overwhelmed me. I was then tested for the Epstein-Barr Virus (mononucleosis) and it was determined that I had chronic EBV. As symptoms persisted, Chronic Fatigue Syndrome, or CFS, was diagnosed.

Feeling sick and tired most of the time, I wondered, "Was I going to be chronically fatigued all of my life?" This diagnosis felt like a prison sentence to me. The news was very depressing, not to mention trying to explain this baffling condition. I felt terribly misunderstood and alone. This was not just fatigue. I found out that people who have CFS are often misjudged by others. There were even instances where I felt judged by my own family. In defense of all my CFS friends, I believe that unless diagnosed with this, one cannot fully comprehend how disabling it is.

Because my symptoms were on the extreme end of the spectrum, an internist ran all sorts of tests, looking for more definitive answers. From dengue fever to Lyme disease, I became a blood donor, so to speak, as vials and vials of my blood were taken. In the meantime, I wondered when this nightmare would end.

The mental battle was intense. I would tell myself, "You really aren't sick – snap out of it!" It was so hard for me to accept that I was not healthy and might always be in this state. Fatigue doesn't begin to describe this complex immune disorder. You feel as if you have the flu most every day or that you have taken a bottle of muscle relaxers, yet still have to function. Deep inside, I felt that maybe the doctors were missing something.

At one point, they administered antiviral I.V. medications. I had a pik line inserted in my upper arm and eventually a central line placed in my chest to pump in the medications. I felt like a human guinea pig, wanting desperately to be well. I fell into despair frequently, but thankfully, Jesus picked me up and put me back on my feet again and again. The little strength I had was firmly in Christ, and I knew He could be trusted.

I read the Bible daily in order to cope, and prayed, begging God to heal me. I leaned heavily on my family and our church during this difficult time. The Lord was slowly teaching me to die to myself and to let go of my dreams and hopes of what I thought life should be. Little by little, he taught me to let go of Angie's agenda and plans as well. My prayer had always been, "Here I am Lord, send me" but did I really know what I was praying?

I grew up singing the hymn "I Surrender All." Did I understand the words that I sang? Definitely not... but God knew my heart and He knew I was willing.

Even though the storm continued to blow from all directions, I found solace in the scriptures, and I knew from my past that I could trust Him with my future.

Chapter 4

In the Eye of the Storm

We have this hope as an anchor for the soul, firm and secure. (Hebrews 6:19)

The summer of 2000 found me weak, pale and thin. I was sliding downhill fast and prayed for the Lord to grab hold of me. The internist sent me to a rheumatologist who diagnosed mixed connective tissue disease or MCTD. This is a maddening diagnosis for the patient because any one of these auto-immune diseases, such as lupus, scleroderma or rheumatoid arthritis, can erupt at any time. Simultaneously, I was diagnosed with fibromyalgia, which is a muscle disorder that causes pain, insomnia, and depression. These new diagnoses left me devastated.

Bone numbing weakness drained me of strength, and I pled with God to sustain me for the sake of my babies, who were only two and three years old at the time. I weighed less than 100 pounds and it looked like I was waiting to die. Hope was fading fast.

"Surely the arm of the Lord is not too short to save, nor his ear too dull to hear" (Isaiah 59:1). He changes times and seasons. He rescues, and He saves. His eye is on His children, as He comforts and delivers us in the most unexpected ways. God was about to send a break in the clouds.

One day the Lord surprised me by sending a beautiful red cardinal to my house. This handsome bird would sit on the power lines in our back yard and sing when I was feeling my worst. Through the arched window in our living room I could see him from the couch where I lay. He was my little encourager. During this same time, "His eye is on the Sparrow" was sung at our church, and my aunt Margie sent me a book titled "And I Know He Watches Me." The Lord was reminding me that His eye was on His child.

No matter what your circumstances look like, His eye is fixed upon you! There is One who cares for you and loves you. The Bible says that the Lord will never leave you, or forsake you. (Hebrews 13:5) My friend, He has not forgotten you. God made no mistake when He knit you together in your mother's womb. He is for you and not against you, and He still performs miracles today.

This little red bird became a daily reminder to me of the Savior who cared about me, and with his daily visits, I felt the love of the Lord. To this day, whenever I see a red cardinal, I am reminded of this encounter that took place several years ago.

I decided to name my feathered friend "Hope" because his song gave me hope, that God was near and aware of my frail condition. Often I would be lying down due to overwhelming weakness, and without fail, here would come his song. I was deeply comforted by God's tenderness. "Hope" stayed near our house for months, and I'm sure he must have been relieved when he got another assignment.

Call me crazy, but I believe that God dispatched that bird to my address. We serve a personal God who is found even in the small stuff. In James 1:17 it states, *"Every good and perfect gift is from above, coming down from the Father of lights...* " Well, that bird was a good gift sent to encourage me, and he certainly came from above! I even took a picture of "Hope" perched on the power lines where we always saw him.

Greg and the children became aware of my bird and how he sang multiple times during the day. The bird's shrill whistle grated on my husband. He was not so grateful for "Hope" because his loud whistle was our alarm clock every morning. I have vivid memories of our cardinal waking us at 5am (we thought that he was part rooster)! Greg would moan and throw two pillows over his head saying he wished he could shoot the bird. Thank goodness we lived in the city. I, too, became annoyed at the 5am wake-up call, but for me, "Hope" was still a reminder of an ever-present God in my time of trouble.

Throughout this illness, the Lord has comforted me so much through His creation. From a child's smile to a snail, I see God in everything. I especially like birds, and bird watching has become a hobby of mine. I'm fascinated by their freedom to fly. It reminds me of a verse in Psalm 55:6 where David writes, *"Oh, that I had the wings of a dove! I would fly away and be at rest."* Wouldn't we all like to do that at times in our lives?

Even as I write this, God is using the cardinal to encourage me once again. Lately, constant migraines have worn me out. Then I developed bronchitis, and while coughing, fractured a rib. Awful depression set in as a result of the new and constant pain. However, my Father in heaven knew I was downhearted, and for a month now, I have been getting daily cardinal reminders. Two days after I fractured my rib, a very close friend came to my house wearing a beautiful grey sweater with a red cardinal right in the center of it! Tears welled up in my eyes as I thanked the Lord, and hope sprung alive in my heart again.

Getting back to the story, as my health declined, our doctor was now recommending a hysterectomy. With each monthly cycle came a flare of all the other symptoms. We sought a second opinion and the other physician agreed. I remember crying at the appointment. Greg and I prayed for wisdom and direction and asked God to direct our steps as we waited to make the decision.

Finally, my little feathered friend flew away and I began to feel alive again. Food sounded good to me and I slowly started to gain weight. The winds of the storm began to die down, and calmness prevailed. My hair stopped falling out and I gained strength as the shroud of illness that covered me like a heavy blanket began to lift. I found it easy to smile, and we even had family pictures made. I felt fantastic, thanking God every minute for the reprieve. To my complete surprise, I began to have some of those familiar, "motherly" symptoms… and my intuition was right. No wonder I was crying, not ready for a hysterectomy…I was pregnant! Don't you love quick answers to prayer? The Lord indeed answered our prayers in the most wonderful and unexpected way!

We were elated and anxious at the same time. The doctors said it was probable that I would miscarry due to antibodies detected prior to pregnancy. I am so glad that God holds the answers. He knows the end from the beginning. With Him nothing is too difficult. He holds the keys to life and death and it was His will for this new little life to bring us joy! Greg and I thanked God profusely for this little baby in my womb. Happiness filled me as I witnessed a miracle.

All these changes were a breath of fresh air for me and my family. Taking advantage of this time, I felt so healthy that we went on a vacation to Disney World. I was astounded that I could walk the entire park on my own two legs and keep up with my family. I pushed my three and five year-olds around in a double-wide stroller and I didn't once have to ride in it. We had an incredible time, and I even rode a small roller coaster!

"Is this what it feels like to be alive?" was a frequent thought. Yes, the burden of illness had been lifted! Oh, how I long for that again. I had truly been rescued by this baby. What a divine and beautiful plan that only God could have orchestrated.

I enjoyed decorating the baby's room and was even able to do aerobics throughout most of the pregnancy. What a far cry from months before when I could barely make it up our stairs. I'll never forget that precious time of "normalcy." I was cooking for my family, playing with my children and shopping to make up for lost time. I did not take even one of those days for granted.

Eventually, we found out we would be having another little girl so we chose the name "Emma," which means "healing" or "wholeness." This pregnancy had pushed the disease into remission, making me feel healed, wonderful and whole.

By the eighth month, a familiar exhaustion returned. I could not stay awake, and something felt amiss. My doctor found that Epstein-Barr virus was active again, so I was placed on antiviral medications and was given orders to rest. Even though the doctor told me the chances were slim, I worried that I'd pass this virus to my unborn baby. The upcoming delivery also brought fear because of the traumatic experience with my second child. I tried to rest in God, daily placing this tiny life in my womb in His competent hands.

Our enemy, Satan, loves to bring the past to our minds, tormenting us with it. I love the verse, "*...Forgetting what is* *behind and straining toward what is ahead, I press on toward the goal to win the prize for which God has called me heavenward in Christ Jesus"* (Philippians 3:13-14). God was teaching me to put the past behind me, and to have faith, not fear.

This reminds me of the time, further ahead in the story, when I was waiting to get a bone marrow biopsy, which I dreaded terribly. The name itself made me cringe. As my husband escorted me to this "torture" clinic, a man with leukemia sat down beside me. Apparently he could see the troubled look on my face. It was my first biopsy, and I was petrified, to say the least. I would be wide awake for this procedure, and it sounded like pure agony. He shared with me that he had endured twenty-five such biopsies, so I guess you could say he was an "expert" at this. He looked me in the eye, saying something I will not ever forget. He said, "Faith is much easier than fear." I was able to exhale after this precious man shared those words of wisdom with me. Isn't that how God would have us look at life?

We've heard it a million times. Ninety percent of what we worry about never even happens. I confess, I'm guilty of this worry and have to ask God daily to renew my mind, to forgive me and help me to meditate on what I know to be true. As it says in Philippians 4:8, *"Finally, brothers, Whatever is true, whatever is noble, whatever is right, whatever is pure, whatever is lovely, whatever is admirable– if anything is excellent or praiseworthy– think about such things."*

It turned out that all my worry was time wasted because my delivery went very smoothly, praise God. Emma Rose came into the world a beautiful, healthy little girl. She was such a special blessing and we all adored her. I held and rocked this baby as much as possible, treasuring every moment.

A peculiar thing began to happen, though, right after her birth. The Lord kept reminding me of Joshua 1:9, *"Be strong and courageous. Do not be terrified; do not be discouraged, for the LORD your God will be with you wherever you go."* Numerous times, through different sources, God confirmed this verse to me. I began to think, "Lord, what is about to happen?" I felt uneasiness in my spirit for weeks. I knew the Lord was trying to warn me of something. Naturally, I thought that something was going to happen to *me*.

When my baby was six weeks old, the twin towers of the World Trade Center fell following a terrorist attack in New York City (September 11, 2001). Was God trying to comfort me with the verse about what was about to happen? Evidently He did not want me to be afraid. The verse stopped coming to my mind after the tragedy. Two weeks later, Emma developed pneumonia and was hospitalized at Texas Children's Hospital in the Houston medical center. Now I had to trust that God would heal my newborn. After all, she was His child on loan to me and He was her heavenly Father. If He threw the stars out into space and formed the universe, He could heal my baby of pneumonia. God heard our prayers and Emma recovered, but she had to have breathing treatments frequently.

We were so grateful for this child because she had given my tired body and soul a break from illness.

To my dismay, my body began to return to its old ways. Even while nursing I had monthly cycles that would bring on a flare of weakness and pain. I did not want a hysterectomy, however this is what was being recommended once again. Greg and I covered this decision in much prayer and consulted with four separate doctors this time for their opinions.

Surprisingly, they all agreed on the surgery. We truly thought it would help because I felt wonderful when pregnant with no menstrual cycles. It was a difficult decision to make, to say the least.

The morning of my surgery, God wrapped me in a blanket of the most amazing peace. I even woke up singing before we drove to the hospital. After the hysterectomy, I felt great for several months. My energy returned and I even adjusted to immediate menopause with no major bumps. But, as anyone who has weathered a major storm can tell you, after the peaceful calm of the eye passes, the storm's fury returns once again. So I'm sure you can understand how distressed I was when my health started to slip downhill, all over again...

Chapter 5

The Medical Maze

My soul finds rest in God alone; my salvation comes from him. He alone is my rock and my salvation; He is my fortress, I will never be shaken. (Psalm 62:1-2)

After a very brief reprieve, my body started to present all kinds of bizarre signals that things were growing worse. I lost stamina, and the weakness and fatigue were now joined by a new companion—pain. Even though I was so tired of having my life consumed by all things "medical," some problems became so intense that I had no choice but to seek treatment.

Over time, new symptoms developed and others changed. Often Greg and I believed that we had found a diagnosis only to find out that it was incorrect. I would sometimes be given medications or other treatments that would backfire, landing me in an emergency room or back home in even more pain than before. We finally said, "That's it! We are going to stay away from doctors and ride this out." And we did just that, until intense pain, or other alarming symptoms drove us back.

Exhausted by physicians' never-ending attempts to help, I turned to alternative medicine. A small fortune was spent at health food stores and on a variety of "holistic" professionals who offered help in non-traditional ways. While some things did help, the overall situation continued to worsen with no real lasting relief.

In all honesty, I believe I've tried enough pills, powders, juices, creams, patches, oils, vitamins, minerals and herbs to fill a dump truck! In the early years I had more hope in doctors, medicines and miracle supplements. Although some offered help, most did not. I was sent to every kind of "ologist" imaginable to help make sense of the madness. Due to the complexity of my case, I was led to doctor after doctor and test after test with confusion surrounding me on every side. It seemed like I was a puzzle that was missing a few pieces.

One doctor said I had "fleas and ticks", meaning that there was more than one disease process going on. Another doctor compared me to a yellow canary. I liked the canary comparison better. I wrestled with the medicines, hating them but needing them. I feared getting hooked on them, and dreamed of flushing them.

I endured painful acupuncture or "acu-torture" as I called it, three times a week for 6 months. And as I write this, I'm trying another round of acupuncture for pain relief. I wore magnets and had special foot baths to draw out toxins. Carrots, celery and spinach were juiced for breakfast, and I drank herbal tea at night. I used aromatherapy and even rubbed "horse cream" on my inflamed feet (amazing stuff by the way). Steroid creams were applied to swollen joints and steroid drops were placed in my inflamed eyes. Then there were the pain patches, nitroglycerin patches, estrogen patches and earplugs (the latter was needed in order to survive my snoring husband).

One night, exhausted from the day's events, I walked from the living room to the bedroom with my pills in one hand and my earplugs in the other. Not knowing if I was coming or going, I popped the earplugs in my mouth instead of the pills!

Of course, I promptly spit the earplugs across the room. Then there was a brief time where I had to wear nitroglycerin patches due to coronary spasms. During this phase of treatment, I was supposed to take the nitroglycerin patch off in the middle of the night, but unknown to me, I took off my estrogen patch instead, and my man woke up with it stuck to his head! At one point, he made a chart so I would know when to take what. Poor Greg, it unnerved him that I could not be "fixed," and as my husband and caregiver, he felt completely helpless.

Syndromes, viruses and diseases were diagnosed one by one, and it became hard for me to believe they all could all reside in my five-foot frame.

Irritable bowel was found first causing duodenal wall spasms. This was later diagnosed as a motility disorder or gastroparesis. Next came fibromyalgia, systemic lupus (SLE), Sjogren's syndrome, osteoporosis and interstitial cystitis. Mitral valve prolapse, asthma and rheumatoid arthritis were recently diagnosed as well. In addition to all this, add five bulging discs, neuropathies, food allergies, and depression (no surprise there).

As you can imagine the range of symptoms was overwhelming and without God's grace and strength I would not have been able to bear it. I live with constant stomach pain, back pain, chest pain, fatigue, weakness, arthritis, hair loss, dry eyes and mouth as well as frequent headaches, bladder spasms, dizziness, brain fog and shortness of breath.

I can guess what you are probably thinking by now, and I assure you, I am not a hypochondriac. I've discovered that there are many others out there suffering, whose medical situations don't fit inside "the box." Because of their limitations, society has kicked them to the curb, so to speak, or has stigmatized them with statements like "it's all in your head," or "you're just depressed."

After the birth of my third child, I began to have heart issues. Painful coronary spasms, mimicking a heart attack, sent me to the hospital several times. An EKG showed pericarditis (inflammation around the heart), which is a hallmark of lupus. Since my symptoms were at the severe end of chronic fatigue syndrome, the internist said that we needed to check for specific lupus anti-bodies. Here is an excerpt from my journal describing that night.

April 6, 2004

Tonight at about 9:00 p.m., I called to get the results of recent lab work. Dialing my special patient number, I anxiously awaited to hear a recorded message about my results. Even though they have repeatedly checked for lupus, I was still not prepared to hear the doctor's message. She said that for the first time she sees definitive signs of lupus. I had three antibody tests, specific for lupus, and they all came back positive.

Motioning my husband to come, I nervously pressed #1 again so he could hear the message. We were speechless. We finally had an answer, but not one that anyone would want. I went to sit down in the living room with my mom and Greg and began to cry. My husband, who had been so overwhelmed and weary, kissed me on the head and went to the bedroom. I thought maybe he needed time to process this disturbing news. So my Mom and I talked for a little while and cried together. What a blessing my mother has been, putting her life on hold while serving my family. She needed rest so I decided to go check on Greg because he has described himself lately as being numb. While he has been worried about me, I have been worried about him. I quietly opened the door to find him snoring. I smiled and thanked God that he was sleeping. It was 11:00 p.m. by this time, and I needed to still my heart before attempting to sleep on the news that had just been given to me. I decided to write for the next hour.

Opening my journal, I felt lonely and sad about my situation. There is no cure for lupus. Would I battle this serious disease for the rest of my life? My eyes then glanced at the scripture at the bottom of the journal page. In this notebook, every page had a different verse on the bottom. It read, *"The LORD will fight for you; you need only to be still"* (Exodus 14:14). Completely amazed, I sat motionless in pure awe of my Father in heaven! After about five minutes of silence, I began to sing, "I stand, I stand in awe of you"…tears…"I stand, I stand in awe of you"…more tears…"Holy God to whom all praise is due, I stand in awe of you." I then found my Bible and turned to Exodus 14:14 to find out more about this beautiful verse of scripture. Joy overwhelmed me because this verse was speaking about the parting of the Red Sea!

My eight year old son has been fascinated ever since he heard the story of Moses leading the people out of Egypt. In fact, he has been drawing pictures of Moses and the parting sea for more than a year now.

The pieces were coming together, as I realized that God was speaking to my heart through the drawings of my child and His Word.

Somehow, with what I have been shown tonight, God will deliver me.

To me, this story demonstrates just how real God is. God's attention to timing and details is astounding. Dear friend, if you are facing a serious disease, a bad report or the unknown; seek the Lord and His strength. He is the Lord, and there is no other (Isaiah 45:5). He defends all who come to Him for protection (Proverbs 30:5). *"The LORD is close to the brokenhearted and saves those who are crushed in spirit"* (Psalm 34:18).

To this day, I am allotted a thimble-full of energy; thus I have to choose my priorities carefully. Have you ever wanted a bed that lifts you up and dumps you out? I sure did. Most days it demands every ounce of me to shift from "park" into "drive" and still I feel like I'm stuck in "neutral!" It seemed that my vocation was studying ceiling fans and finding shapes in the spackling. I'm sure some of you can identify, and have mastered these skills as well.

On the worst days, I could not get out of bed. Sometimes, it is a huge accomplishment just to unload the dishwasher or wash my hair, and still others I would have to sit down to rest after sweeping the kitchen floor. On my bad days, I am like a dog on a tight leash, and when released (as in a break in symptoms) boy can I run! Running for me is going out to eat, and shopping in the evening at just one store.

I was, and still am terrible at pacing myself, and when I have a slightly good day, I blow my thimble-full and then some. This can throw me in bed for the next day. Balance is something this "all or nothing" girl cannot seem to comprehend.

I have seen over thirty doctors and been a patient in several hospitals in the Houston medical center and elsewhere. My symptoms did not fit the mold, and this was the reason that I was sent from one doctor to the next. A trusted doctor sent me to M.D. Anderson. Then, a few years later, three doctors advised that I go to the Mayo Clinic. I wanted to live a "normal" life as a wife and mother, but my poor health simply would not allow it. Having endless medical tests or spending hours in waiting rooms and seeing scores of doctors was not how I wanted to live.

To make matters worse, a few doctors I saw were rude and even verbally abusive. Early on, I felt sick, with few blood markers, so I had to present my case defending myself. I walked into many appointments consumed with physical pain and left feeling emotionally beaten and spiritually downcast. My case became incredibly challenging with multiple chemical sensitivities and contraindications. More often than not, my body responded to strong medications with toxic, allergic or rare reactions. And, as if it were my fault, these doctors would then get irritated and some took out their frustration on me.

Once while hospitalized, a rheumatologist had the gall to make fun of me because of my sensitive stomach, (he did this at 6:00 a.m. in front of the nurse, while I lay helpless in bed). Another asked me if I had looked in the mirror lately. I had been having unrelenting headaches, so naturally I did not look like a beauty queen. As a result of those experiences, I developed bitterness toward doctors that I later had to repent of. Sadly, some completely forget there is a person attached to the disease.

On the bright side, there were kind doctors who treated me with compassion and respect. Words of comfort coming from a doctor are consoling to those who face a life-threatening illness. The tongue is powerful, speaking words of life or death. Friends, we must remember that doctors are imperfect people who make mistakes. They are not gods. I came to realize that doctors are men and women with big band-aids whom God can definitely use to carry out His will.

Not long after the lupus diagnosis, I was sent to M. D. Anderson Cancer Center for six months of outpatient treatment. Because of some very specific symptoms, cancer doctors believed I had either a rare blood disease called mastocytosis, or neuroendocrine tumors. I arrived at the leukemia department once a week for blood tests. Needless to say, this was a nerve-racking time. I was enrolled in a clinical trial, taking a leukemia drug that helped diseases like the one they suspected I had. But I was eventually removed from the trial because of a toxic reaction that I had to the drug. Given that both of these diseases were extremely rare, one doctor said that he wished he could put me in a glass box and observe me. I didn't know whether to laugh or cry. Thankfully, it was later determined I did not have either of these diseases.

Oncologists put me through the mill, testing me for several types of cancer, along with grueling tests like bone marrow biopsies. I was checked for pancreatic cancer, bone cancer and leukemia. Osteoporosis was diagnosed during this period, and an endocrinologist informed me that I was at risk for fractures—this was before steroids were ever taken for lupus.

I ached for my youth that had been ripped away; this was a profound loss that I frequently cried over. At age 34, I was post-menopausal and osteoporotic with a handicap placard and a large pill organizer. Oh, and I cannot forget the dreadful support hose that I was supposed to wear for my serious hypotension. I know why they tell you to put these on daily because the strain involved in stretching them over your feet would raise anyone's blood pressure!

My body was weak, my blood pressure would plummet and fainting was not uncommon. For this reason, I had to rent a wheelchair since I could not walk long distances. Ultimately, we ended up buying one for rare trips to the mall. (Praise God, it now sits in a corner of our garage with an old towel thrown over it.) At the time, I was in my thirties with three children at home. I struggled to identify with my peers, and quite frankly, I envied those with health like my active mom and husband who ran circles around me. I needed perspective, so God used my weekly trips to the cancer center to teach me that, and much more.

Traveling the halls of a cancer center, and seeing the pain on cancer-stricken faces, will change you forever. My problems, though disabling, somehow seemed smaller; and in time, I came to identify with these extraordinary people because they, too, knew what it was like to suffer. You can learn a lot about perseverance from one living with cancer. From this experience, I was able to share with many patients about the love of Jesus, and my faith grew as I walked through the fire. Just five years earlier, I had walked these familiar halls holding my dad's hand, and now someone else was holding mine.

To preface this next journal entry, I'd had a CT scan of my kidneys due to several small kidney stones; however, in the process, a bone lesion was found on my femur. The urologist sent me to my rheumatologist who subsequently referred me to an oncologist who then determined a bone scan was needed. That bone scan was the reason for my second stint at the cancer center. In this journal entry I describe one of my days:

May 13, 2004

Today is bone scan day at M.D. Anderson Cancer Center and Greg is exhausted. He has seldom missed an appointment in all these years, so today he is letting my friend drive me for testing. I'm thankful for this because he truly needs a break. My friend has done many loving things like bringing me cut flowers from her garden and cooking our family special meals. I'll never forget the time she took my sick and deformed African violet home with her. It had serious problems and grew off to one side, leaning horizontally instead of vertically. Only God knew that it bugged me the way this flower grew, and that I wanted it fixed. She repotted it for me, and for a while, it still looked dreadful (I even put it outside because it was an eyesore). Eventually it straightened some, although still slightly crooked; now it blooms! This unique violet makes me smile. I am thankful for the friends who have helped me out with the details of life. Farfetched as this may be, this violet is a lot like me. I started out growing toward the sun, and in my upward course, the body took a detour. It didn't bloom when it was off course; in fact, it became sick, until the gardener turned it upside down and repotted it.

Now getting back to my appointment, as we made our way to nuclear medicine, I was apprehensive because they had to inject me with radioactive dye. I'm terribly tired of needles and I.V.'s. I've gotten somewhat used to them, but they still hurt. God tested me on this particular day in a way I could have never expected. After two hours of waiting for the dye to get in my bloodstream, it was time for me to be scanned. Several of us were sitting in the holding room awaiting our turn. The technician called my name and instructed me to lie down. Bone scans are scary because they are primarily looking for bone cancer, which is what I was being checked for. The scan is from head to toe and is nothing like a bone density scan. I had to lie flat on the table with my head turned to one side while a heavy piece of metal, as big as my kitchen table, moved ever so slowly until it reached my toes. I must add that it was lowered within 1 inch of me! I felt like the middle of a sandwich. The frightening part came when my scan was over and the technician was now staring at my bones on a monitor. He proceeds to ask me if the doctor is looking at my head. I replied, "No, the suspicious area is my right thigh." By this point, I was not feeling at ease. He looked at me and said in his Indian accent, "We must repeat the test." Little did I know, God was about to give me a test – a big one! The technician now had me staring straight ahead at the heavy metal plank one inch from my nose. Fear began to sweep over me as I said to myself, "I don't need to worry about the bone lesion on my leg – there's something wrong with my brain!" I closed my eyes and asked God to take away the fear that had invaded my mind. He did, and I continued to pray silently telling the Lord that I wanted Him to be glorified in me. I went on to tell the Lord that I was here to serve Him in whatever way that meant. The quiet voice of the Lord stunned me by asking a question. *"Would you even die for me?"* (Now, remember, I am staring at a two-ton piece of machinery designed to look for bone cancer with a technician sitting beside me who has just asked me if the doctors are looking at my head.) I hesitated for about two seconds wondering if the metal monster was going to malfunction which would be the death of me! I then replied, "Yes Lord, I would even die for you."

The radiology report showed that I had an osteolytic lesion – which often means cancer. Fortunately, after a pretty good scare, it was diagnosed as benign.

Speaking of tests, I got weary of them and became sick of them. I wanted my life to consist of more than doctor appointments and tests. The medical maze took many twists and turns as I battled a disease that affected many body parts and systems. With a complex set of syndromes and diseases, it seemed I was placed on a medical "merry-go-round."

More than once I was sent on a medical goose chase. For instance, I would be at the rheumatologist with shortness of breath, and I would get sent to the pulmonologist who would do breathing tests. When the test results were inconclusive, I was sent to the neurologist, and then further scans were scheduled. This process was grueling, as I describe in this next entry:

January 17, 2005

What a long, intense day of tests, waiting and more tests. My dear mom drove to Houston to take me to St. Luke's Hospital. I am glad once again that Greg gets a break. Today I am struggling with strong fatigue, wishing I could stay home with my kids who have a holiday from school. Unfortunately, illness takes no holiday.

It saddens me to see their little hands wave to me over the short fence in our breezeway as we drive away. Sometimes this all seems to be a horrible waste of time and money.

The gallium scan went smoothly, no needles, yeah! After we were done the technician came to get me for one more scan, a lateral view of the lungs. Then you are left to worry, until you receive a report from the doctor. Or trust in the Lord and rest in Him…something I am working on.

Our day went downhill after lunch. We took the walk from the hospital to the towers and checked in at the lobby for the CT scan. The lobby was a huge open area. I scoped out the chairs, and found a comfy leather one calling my name, so I settled in closing my weary lids. About ten minutes later a woman sat down on the other side of my mom. She was handicapped in several ways, and it appeared that she had a type of palsy. She was also partially deaf and began to talk to herself. It was obvious that she did not want to be here, so Mom kindly told her that God would take care of her. Probably because of the hearing difficulty, she spoke loudly, and sitting on the edge of her seat with a raised voice she asked, "Where is God?"

I sank in my chair thinking, "Please Lord, help, I'm too tired for this today." Then she spoke even louder, "Where did he come from?" My mother gently said that He is a supreme being in heaven. The lady replied, "Aren't we cells that spontaneously formed?" I shook my head no, now wanting to help this confused lady. Before I could say any more she raised her voice another notch, "The Bible is just a book written by men!" We told her it was the inspired Word of God. She shook her head no. Mom said, "We have to believe that God is who he said He is." I added that we accept this by faith. She looked annoyed at us even though we spoke to her with gentleness and love.

About this time a gentlemen called me back to a cubicle several yards away, however, still in earshot. Half of me had a hard time leaving Mom in the heat of this Bible battle, while the other half of me sighed in relief to be able to leave the scene. I tried to pray for them in between answering insurance questions. Then, above all the other chatter I heard, "YOU'RE UPSETTING ME!" I recognized the voice, thinking, "Oh no, I've got to rescue Mother!" Thankfully, I was finished checking in, so I hurried over to check on my mom. She had a worn-out look on her face and was standing by the elevators looking for a way of escape. She was relieved to hear that we had to go to another floor to wait in yet another waiting room.

But before we left the floor, I felt the Lord speaking to my heart about leaving this woman a gospel tract. I was a little afraid to walk over to her, but knew that God was asking me to. She was still sitting in the same chair. Feeling compelled, I hugged her saying, "God loves you; He will show you the truth."

I then changed into a gown with the words "Hospital Property" written all over it in various colors. Like I would try to escape with this beautiful gown? The long narrow holding area had chairs lined up by a wall of windows where about ten people were waiting for IV's and scans. This turned out to be a long two hour wait. There was a vast array of personalities, all waiting their turn, just like me. On my left was a doctor with cancer, and a sleeping flight attendant. On my right was a woman from Mexico City, waiting with her husband who had cancer. Her eyes were sad, and it looked as if she had been crying. Then there was an elderly woman who was talking 90 miles an hour to a lady next to her who had a cold. A very thin woman, about my age sat next to her. At the very end, sitting by himself was a frail old man with a wet hand towel draped over his head with eyes fixed straight ahead. He could not have weighed more than 70 pounds and looked terribly sick. As I listened to the conversations, and in talking with a few of them, it was very clear to me that I was the only one with real hope. The words of Jesus came quickly to my mind, "...*The harvest is plentiful but the workers are few*"(Matthew 9:37).

How I want to be one of God's workers. I believe that the harvest is indeed ready, but sadly, some of us are preoccupied.

The doctor was a sophisticated older man who had lung cancer. I asked him what it was like on the other side, and he stated that it was not fun at all. I felt sad for him, not knowing what to say (doctors get sick too, and are not immune from disease). He did not acknowledge God in our conversation and later I regretted that I did not tell him about Jesus. After he left, I tried to be more diligent with the opportunity I had been given.

By this time, my IV had been placed, and it was almost my turn to be scanned. I was tired. Looking up from my magazine, the deaf woman, with whom we had a confrontation with earlier, came walking down the narrow hall. I then prayed, "Lord, will this day ever end?"I instinctively shrunk back until she walked right up to me, telling me that she was afraid of CT scans. I tried to calm her by telling her that I'd had lots of scans, and that they were pretty easy. Right away she said, "I need a nurse!"Bless her heart, she asked the nurse if the staples would come out of her ears during the CT scan, and what should she do with her teeth. My heart filled with compassion for this afflicted one.

Finally it was time for my scan, and by this time, I was absolutely delighted to lie down in the darkened room...alone. After the scan was done, and the IV catheter was removed, I felt extremely nauseous and faint. My blood pressure had hit the floor, and I had to lie down for a while before I could get up. Finally, I was stable enough to walk, so slowly I made my way to the lockers to retrieve my clothes. I looked up to see the frail man, with the green rag still draped over his head, sitting in the same chair. I just could not walk past him like he wasn't there. I felt drawn to this poor soul. Putting my hands on top of his, I told him that Jesus really loved him, and I hugged his bony frame. This sweet man looked up at me with a warm toothless smile. He genuinely thanked me and as I walked away, tears streamed down my cheeks. Something within me wanted to take this little forgotten man home with me, and take care of him. That "something"was the love of Christ.

I left the hospital that day emotionally, physically, and spiritually spent. On the drive home, a cloud of depression hung over me, along with a pounding headache and stomach ache. My thoughts were negative, thinking that my life consisted of running to doctors and hospitals and enduring endless tests. Arriving home, I made a beeline for the bedroom, where I promptly got in bed, clothes and all. I could not rest, though, because of the worsened headache and burning chest pain. I felt I would throw up at any minute. Seeing my state, Greg called our neighbor to see if she had any nausea medicine. Can you believe God placed a Christian counselor three doors down the street? Sally came with the medicine and asked Greg if she could pray for me. He let her come to my bedside where I told her briefly of the heavy burdens of the day, and as she prayed I sobbed into my pillow. She reminded me that God did not design us to carry other people's burdens. Sally was a huge comfort that night and stayed for a little while holding my hand.

Suffering friends, I understand how disabling a chronic illness can be. Although they come in many different shapes and sizes, there are some common denominators, such as pain and fatigue. Pain can paralyze even the most active person. It wrings you out leaving you exhausted and undone. It can also cause irritability and depression. My heart is so tender for those of you who are in despair right now over the loss of your health and those struggling with pain. I know exactly how weary you are. Don't lose hope, dear one; you are not alone. You, too, can have peace in the midst of pain. Call on Jesus. Only in Him can we find the rest we need.

> *Come to me, all you who are weary and burdened, and I will give you rest. Take my yoke upon you and learn from me, for I am gentle and humble in heart, and you will find rest for your souls. For my yoke is easy and my burden is light.* (Matthew 11:28-30)

Chapter 6

Trapped by the Sun

No words can express how much the world owes to sorrow. Most of the Psalms were born in a wilderness. Most of the Epistles were written in a prison. The greatest thoughts of the greatest thinkers have all passed through the fire. Take comfort afflicted Christian! When God is about to make preeminent use of a man He puts him in the fire.[1]
– George MacDonald

One morning, looking out my kitchen window, I noticed that a sparrow had crawled into the feeding tube of our bird feeder. My husband and I could not imagine how it squeezed under the small opening. Feeling sorry for him, I went outside in my pink bathrobe to see this small bird wildly flapping about trying to escape the confines of the tube. Knowing just how he felt, I couldn't wait to set him free. The bird reminded me of my own confinement. Tearfully, I unscrewed the lid on top of the feeder and without hesitation he flew away to freedom.

I made a connection with the sparrow that day, only in my case I cannot simply fly away. For years I have felt confined, trapped and imprisoned in a body that constantly works against me. I've wished many days that I could unzip my sick body and trade it in for a healthy one. The overwhelming feeling of confinement developed because the sun has hemmed me in. I'm ensnared by a powerful force that is absolutely vital to survival.

How do you live in a world where the sun comes up every morning and you have to constantly avoid it to live? For those who are photosensitive, that is precisely what you have to do. In systemic lupus, the sunlight can trigger the body to attack itself. Try explaining that to your friends and family! I found this out the hard way after collapsing from spending thirty minutes in my small flower garden.

April 14, 2004

I woke up very weak today but that is not unusual. My morning routine is the same: I roll out of bed slowly because the blood pressure is unstable and my legs are weak; then, I hobble to the kitchen and mix my green vitamin drink, shaking some salt into it to lift up the blood pressure. Mary said to me yesterday, "Mommy, you should be a fish in the ocean since you like salt water so much." I corrected her saying that I did not like salt water, but that the doctor needs me to drink it to keep from fainting."

Every morning, I feel drawn outside to sit on the back porch, thanking God for another day of life.

Unless the weather is bad, I walk to the garden in my pajamas and my husband's large flip-flops. This garden is only 4ft. by 8ft. but oh what therapy it has been for me. It was supposed to have been Greg's tomato garden, but slowly I have stolen it, planting flowers and herbs instead. Nature draws me so close to the Father who made heaven and Earth. This small wood- framed garden becomes my altar, as I pray, pulling weeds and pinching off dead blooms. It has become a special part of my day.

Since my life is at a standstill, I appreciate the little things. Sometimes, I'll watch a spider spin his intricate web, or study the smallest flower with all its detail, and marvel at the dew that sparkles like diamonds on the petals of a rose. This all makes me smile in wonder at our awesome God!

The sun was especially bright this April morning, and as I walked back to the house I felt weaker and weaker with each step. Barely making my way inside, I found the couch, threw a blanket over my legs and closed my eyes. The next thing I remember was hearing my husband tell Matthew that his mommy needed a hug. I saw my son and could hear his voice clearly, but for the life of me, I could not move or even speak.

Greg and his mom were extremely concerned and wanted to move me to the bedroom, so he lifted one arm while she lifted the other. They tried to set me on my feet, but my legs and feet would not cooperate. They had no idea my limbs were paralyzed. I distinctly remember having socks on and as they lifted my arms, my feet dragged across the slick wood floor. To me, everything seemed to be moving in slow motion. I heard them speaking, but I could not respond. I thought maybe I'd had a stroke, but there was absolutely no fear.

My husband knelt down beside my bed repeating, "Don't die on me!" I remember wanting to cry, but could not. Then I fell into a very deep sleep (or was unconscious) for about six hours. Upon waking, I got out of bed at a snail's pace, feeling like something had steamrolled me; not knowing what time or even what day it was. I stumbled to the kitchen where my worried mother-in-law brought soup to the table. Ironically, this verse was at the bottom of my journal page that very day:

The LORD upholds all those who fall and lifts up all who are bowed down." (Psalm 145:14)

The Lord undeniably raised me up that day. When I went to see the rheumatologist the following week, I described to her what had happened and her eyes got as big as saucers. In the most serious tone she said, "The sun is not your friend Angie—it is your enemy."

I was shocked and numb as I swallowed hard trying to digest these life-altering words. Somehow deep in my spirit I knew she was right.

"No, I thought, this cannot be true!" Sadness overwhelmed me as I realized what this meant. Especially since I had promised my children that we would go to the beach that summer. Now, I would not be able to take them anywhere that involved sunshine.

It was explained to me that this unconscious event where I could not talk or move, was life threatening, and that I was lucky to be alive. The cardiologist thought I had an event that mimicked a stroke. He said that I should not have woken up that day. I know that it was not luck, but Jesus who woke me up that day and saved my life once more.

I absolutely love what Dr. John Bisagno said in a sermon once: "We are indestructible until God is finished with us." From my experience, I know this to be true and it's biblical, too.

Photosensitivity or UV light sensitivity is present in about 70 percent of patients with systemic lupus erythematosus (SLE). For some patients, sun exposure, even for as little as thirty minutes, can cause headaches, nausea and joint pain as well as weakness and increased fatigue. I experience all the above symptoms with even minimal exposure. Sun exposure can also cause an increase in the activity of the disease resulting in a flare-up. This may in turn cause an acute attack of inflammation and arthritis, pleurisy (which I encountered frequently), fever, kidney disease, and epilepsy. Doctors believe that the UVA and UVB waves are responsible. Since fluorescent lights emit these same waves many of us (with SLE) have to avoid fluorescent lights as well. And as anyone knows they are everywhere!

At the time of my collapse, I had been experiencing joint pain, nausea, chest pain and weakness with sun exposure. However, I didn't put two and two together until after the event. Sadly, now I knew the cause.

We all know that sunlight is essential for life. No plant can thrive in the absence of light. Trees need it to grow and make oxygen and provide the shade we need. Unless they are shade lovers, flowers need sun in order to bloom; fruits and vegetables ripen in the warm sun, thereby producing our food. Our bodies also need sunlight to produce vitamin D which helps build bones and stabilize our moods. Being a Texan, it is near impossible to escape our hot sun. Even as I write, it is barely June and the temperature has already hit 98 degrees. It looks like we are headed for another scorcher.

The summers have become the season that I dread the most. I have fallen into depression time after time because when I was out in the sun, even for less than thirty minutes, I felt sick. I was trapped by the sun during the day and the increasing pain by night. It has been exasperating to say the least, and there were many moments of intense frustration and sadness over the isolation. It helped me to understand why isolation is used as a form of punishment.

One summer, I was tempted to go out in my backyard and lay out in the sun. I felt like I was nearing the end of my rope. I would look at the doorknob when no one was home and ask God for His strength. It would have been suicide or close to it. This reminds me of the story where Elijah told the Lord, *"I have had enough, LORD," he said. Take my life…"* (1 Kings 19:4).

What kept me from following through was the pain that I would cause my family, and a story that my doctor had told me. She told me about of one of her lupus patients that spent a day at the beach with her kids, and paid dearly for it by spending a whole week in ICU. That picture has been a hard one to shake from my mind. In recent years, I've tried very hard to make the best of things, making lemonade out of the lemons that were handed to me.

Whenever it rains, I receive a "get out of jail free" pass. I am then a caged bird set free! I open all the blinds, and possibly go out for lunch or pick up something I need quickly from the store. What makes shopping tricky for me is that I can no longer linger and enjoy it; I have to hunt and kill it. Men are wired this way, however, I am not.

Since rainy days were good for me, we talked about relocating to the cloudy, rainy city of Seattle, instead of remaining in sizzling South Texas. I now pull weeds and water my flowers in the early morning or evening. Recently, I told my family that I wished that we could all be on the "night shift." Up all night and sleep all day.

I've joked about living underground, or in some sort of space suit that would protect me from radiation. No, I couldn't always make lemonade; it is often a lonely set of circumstances that are very tough to cope with. The Lord was and is my comfort though, and I believe He has cried when I've cried. The Bible says that all our tears are collected in a bottle. Sometimes I wonder if maybe the Lord had to exchange my bottle in for a pitcher.

Many nights I've wept on the back porch as I looked at the stars, wanting the moon to stand still as it did when Joshua prayed. In fact, I have often dreaded the sun coming up and even hated it at times. Sometimes I would fall asleep saddened, because I knew that the next day the sun would rise again and I would be trapped by its forces once more. God definitely had a plan in all this even though, for the life of me, I could not understand this harsh limitation.

Even now, as I write this chapter, I know and trust that Jesus has a purpose for keeping me shut in the house with all the blinds closed. For years I asked and pled with the Lord to remove this barrier, but I believe that God has said, "No", at least for now. At the time of this writing, it has been over five years since that dismal day I was told that the sun was my enemy.

I miss the warmth of the sun on my skin, but I can finally say by God's grace, I have come to accept my strict limitations. I believe with all my heart that the Lord is not holding back anything good from me because, *"The LORD God is a sun and shield; the LORD bestows favor and honor; no good thing does he withhold from those whose walk is blameless"* (Psalm 84:11).

That which is good, in the eyes of a loving God, can look altogether different from our limited vision and comprehension. A trial is often a "good thing", with a purpose to accomplish what the Lord wills. As an example, suppose that in order for this book to be written, the Lord allowed this sun trial so that I would finish writing without distraction? One can sure get a lot of writing done while confined to the home. Nevertheless, I know there are multiple reasons for this complex set of difficulties, and I choose to believe that it must be a good thing to the Lord, or else He would not allow it.

Whatever God is up to, this I know: He loves and cares for me, He does not make mistakes and He can be trusted. He can remove any obstacle in our way in an instant, according to His will. Although many times, He leaves the thorns there so we might learn perseverance. *"Perseverance must finish its work so that you may be mature and complete, not lacking anything"* (James 1:4). As a result, we grow in the Lord, His will is accomplished and He is glorified! We can trust our Father with the details and detours, even when we don't understand why. The Lord will lead us for He is the Shepherd and we are the sheep. I love the times when the Shepherd reveals to His sheep glimpses of the bigger picture as I describe in this next journal entry.

It was a hot August day, when God surprised me with a revelation that knocked my socks off! The Lord was lovingly letting me in on one of His purposes for the sun trial.

August 14, 2006   In Chains for Christ

What a wonderful day, unexpected, but joyous. I have been praying for months that Jesus would give me joy in these dismal circumstances. Struggling with deep despair, I have felt like my life has very little meaning. I find myself thinking of cave dwellers, and wanting to be one of them, to hide from the sun that causes me such pain. Why must my family watch me lie here day after day in pain? I feel lowly in spirit and brokenhearted in a broken body. Within the last week, I shared with some friends through email that I want desperately to rejoice in my suffering and to count it all joy, like the apostle Paul. I want to please my Savior in this way, but joy escapes me. I even told the Lord that this is impossible for me. I felt like I was losing my grip again and slipping back into self-pity.

I decided to go to my desk, looking for a book that I had misplaced, and in the process, I stumbled across an old journal from 1996. I turned to the back of the journal and found where I had scribbled, "Read Philippians every day for 30 days for a thankful heart."Well, I sure could use a thankful heart right now, so I decided to read the four chapters (not knowing that I was being led by the Holy Spirit in doing so).

I grabbed my Bible and crawled into bed, knowing that soon I would have to sleep just to make it through the day. I quickly read chapters 1 through 4 and then went back to the verses in Philippians 1:12-13. These verses had caught my eye, but I began to feel so drowsy that I put my Bible in bed with me, and fell fast asleep. After waking, the first thought on my mind was these verses. I felt the Holy Spirit nudge me, saying that this passage was for me today.

Now I want you to know, brothers, that what has happened to me has really served to advance the gospel. As a result, it has become clear throughout the whole palace guard and to everyone else that I am in chains for Christ. (Philippians 1:12-13)

I am not trying to compare my life to the apostle Paul, but what happened next was an indescribable joy that overwhelmed me. The Lord restored the joy of His salvation! It reminded me of when I was ten years old and had just received Christ. The more I thought about my adversity advancing the gospel, the more I smiled saying, "I'm in chains for Christ. My life does have meaning!" The brightest smile was plastered across my face for a couple of hours, while my family wondered what in the world had come over me.

God knows exactly how we feel and he meets us where we are. He knew how much I needed purpose and meaning at this stage in my race. Oh, how I love my personal Savior! At the end of this beautiful day I prayed:

"Precious Lord, please guard this joy that you have given me, and may I look back on this day and remember how you lifted up my head, telling me I am in chains for your cause, the cause of spreading the gospel."

Chapter 7

Coping

Dealing with a chronic illness can be daunting to say the least. How does one endure a life-threatening disease that constantly changes? There is no doubt that we cope differently based on personality type and life experiences. Without Jesus, I truly don't know how one carries on in the midst of heavy trials. Jesus is my number one way of coping. In fact, *"He is the Way, the Truth and the Life; no man comes to the Father except through Him"* (John 14:6). My relationship and trust in Him is what has carried me through.

This grace and strength that I have found in Jesus Christ has sustained me through years of hardship, and today I cope much better than in the early days. Bad days still come, as diseases like lupus can throw you a curve ball on any given day, but thankfully, I am better at hitting them right to the Lord—casting my cares on Him (1 Peter 5:7). My earnest prayer is that some of my coping methods might help you to survive the chaos that surrounds chronic illness.

In the beginning, it was shock and self-pity that paralyzed me. As a 28-year-old mom, I wanted to be active like all the other young moms. "I'm too young to be sick", I would often think while looking out the window watching everyone going on with their lives. On our busy street, moms were jogging, pushing their toddlers in strollers, or taking their kids to the park, whereas my life was at a standstill.

This kind of inward focus can quickly lead to depression. As I found myself slipping into this trap, the Lord lovingly picked me up, and little by little taught me ways to cope. The Lord used music to encourage me countless times, and it was a welcome distraction from the pain

Praise Music

Music that glorifies God is uplifting and encouraging. My kids grew up with Christian music playing constantly and Mommy singing from the couch. I would tell them that the devil is allergic to praise and believe me, I needed every help possible to keep the enemy from dragging me into the pit. The Psalms show us that God inhabits the praises of His people.

Even in the quiet of the night, while struggling to sleep, the Holy Spirit brought hymns or praise songs to my heart. As I quietly sang, often with tears rolling onto my pillow, the words were a precious reminder of my sustainer and Lord. If too weak, I whispered the ones He brought to mind. These "songs in the night" comforted me in a profound way.

By day the Lord directs his love, at night his song is with me... (Psalm 42:8)

Meditation

Meditation is also a powerful way to cope. Most nights, as I collapsed in the bed not knowing how I could possibly make it through another day, I reflected on Lamentations 3:21-23. *"Yet this I call to mind and therefore I have hope: Because of the LORD's great love we are not consumed, for his compassions never fail. They are new every morning; great is your faithfulness."* I trusted in His faithfulness to give me fresh mercy for the next day, and the Lord never failed once.

This was difficult, especially when depression hit, but it was crucial to train my mind to think positive in the negative situation that surrounded me. I reflected on scripture throughout the day, feeding on it and learning to renew my mind. Here a just a few verses that I meditated on continually:

Set your mind on things above, not on earthly things. " (Colossians 3:2)

And we know that in all things God works for the good of those who love him, who have been called according to his purpose. (Romans 8:28)

I can do everything through him who gives me strength. (Philippians 4:13)

Romans 8:28 is written on my heart, as well as framed on the wall of our home. Through numerous hospital stays, ambulance rides and frantic trips to the emergency room, I prayed for God to show me the good. Sometimes it seemed hard to imagine that anything good would come from the pain and trauma, but knowing that I could trust Jesus and His promises made a world of difference.

Thinking on Heaven

While trying to set my mind on "things above", daydreaming about heaven became yet another way to endure. I found that when we focus on the eternal, it takes our eyes off the temporary. Knowing that my body is just an earthen vessel that will one day be traded in for a new improved body helped me keep a kingdom focus. Reading inspirational books has also provided a much needed escape from the present circumstances.

> *Therefore we do not lose heart. Though outwardly we are wasting away, yet inwardly we are being renewed day by day. For our light and momentary troubles are achieving for us an eternal glory that far outweighs them all. So we fix our eyes not on what is seen, but on what is unseen. For what is seen is temporary, but what is unseen is eternal.* (2 Corinthians 4:16-18)

God's Word

One of the things I treasure most in life is my Bible. I love how the Lord speaks to us and washes us with His life changing words. While I was prescribed numerous medicines for my body, the Psalms were medicine for my soul. I drew lasting comfort in reading one a day.

I believe that these powerful verses were life preservers that kept me from sinking in the fierce storms that raged around me and my family. God's words sustained and fed me – many times I craved them more than food itself. A special time of my day was spent curling up in bed reading my Bible before falling asleep. His law truly is more precious to me than thousands of pieces of silver and gold (Psalm 119:72).

Encouragement

It was suggested to me by a doctor that I needed encouragement for the battle I faced, so he recommended that I read "Streams in the Desert" by L.B. Cowman. I was hospitalized with heart problems the very next week so my husband bought it and delivered it right to my hospital room. Over the years, this book has become like a friend. The words penned have done much more than encourage me, and I have given this book out countless times as gifts.

Encouraging others who are in desperate situations can help to take our eyes off our own physical state. Over time I found this to be a powerful coping method. If I was discouraged I would try to turn my focus to someone else who needed an uplifting word. Ironically, as I looked for a comforting verse, or chose a card for someone else, it would bless and encourage me as well. Just as the proverb says,

>...*he who refreshes others will himself be refreshed*
(Proverbs 11:25).

Support

Encouragement from others lightens the burden of the afflicted. Such life-giving words are like healing balm to the suffering one. Support from others helped me more than I can ever express.

Precious are the ones who take time for the sick. So often, people think that the sick need someone to serve them in some physical way. Recently, I had a friend call me and ask, "What do you need?" My response was that I needed someone to come by for a short visit. I wanted to see someone other than the mailman. While acts of service have blessed me immensely, the presence of a friend taking the time to listen is the most beautiful gift I have received.

These dear ones included a few very close friends and my husband, of course. Then my sweet mother and step-father stood in the gap as did Greg's parents. They were my rescue teams. I don't know what we would have done without their listening ears and servant hearts. They came at a moment's notice to help: cleaning the house, cooking meals, washing mounds of laundry, and taking care of the children. We leaned on them heavily, and they held us up when the burden was too great. Our church was an additional source of support, delivering kids home from school, cooking meals and lifting us up in prayer.

Journaling

Journaling has been said to be quite beneficial in coping. Writing provides a vent, letting off steam that builds up as a result of the frustration surrounding a persistent trial. It was my therapy. When I felt lonely, when no one understood, I'd write. What a faith builder it is to look back on what you've written, and see how God sustained you and answered prayers. Even now, I have a special journal where I write down what God speaks to me. If my house were on fire, this is one of the first things I would grab.

Prayer

Prayer is essential in order to survive a debilitating illness. Through prayer I gained strength and peace, and it also became a way I could quietly serve. From my sickbed or couch, when I could not do something physically for someone, I could pray. God had placed time on my hands—He had set me aside to pray.

Many days I started and ended the day on my knees. My family and I depended on prayer and prayer warriors whom we called on in desperate times. I don't know how we would have endured without this intercession from family and friends. Sometimes it's hard to lay aside our pride and ask for help, especially when dealing with a condition that is ongoing. However, the Bible tells us to carry each other's burdens, and in this way we fulfill the law of Christ (Galatians 6:2). I believe that bearing another's burden is part of God's plan for us as we serve one another. We were not designed to carry our troubles alone.

I know that I have so much more to learn about prayer, but I believe it is beyond awesome that we can bring our requests, pain, and worries before the King of Kings and know that He hears us. Oh, what a privilege! *"...the LORD longs to be gracious to you; he rises to show you compassion; For the LORD is a God of justice. Blessed are all who wait for him!"* (Isaiah 30:18). God answers us from heaven, and He also waits for us to be still. Making time for the Lord in prayer is vital to a closer relationship with Him.

As my relationship with the Lord grew, I became completely dependent on Him, and I watched in awe as He provided for all our needs both great and small. I oftentimes needed to cry out to God in prayer, but because of the unending affliction I just cried a lot, period. Over time though, the frustration and pain need to be released, not internalized, as had been my habit in the past.

Emotional Breakdowns

You might be asking, "How can an emotional breakdown be a way to cope?" In a word – tears. The tears that flowed as a result of these were a release, and thus a way to deal with the pain.

Let me preface this section by saying that my friends and family would characterize me as meek and gentle, and one who does not anger easily. My desire to be transparent places me at risk of being misunderstood, but the Lord wants me to share the truth in hopes that it will help someone else identify.

Along the way, I suffered from several emotional breakdowns which felt like a taste of hell. There were times when I was utterly frustrated with my situation, the disease and the doctors. The breakdowns always happened when I was physically weak, not able to eat, and pain-stricken. They were not pretty. When I felt an episode coming on I would try to work it out myself, pacing with clenched fists in our bedroom saying, over and over, "Jesus help me! As the attack would build, I felt extremely agitated and oppressed, needing my husband to intercede in prayer. One time in particular stands out:

It was a Sunday evening and the kids were watching a "Veggie Tales" movie in our family room while Greg was engrossed at the computer. He was watching the weather, something he loves to do. Ironically, he was closely monitoring a hurricane on the radar. In complete desperation, I marched up to him with my fists still clenched at my sides and said in an angry whisper, "There is a hurricane brewing right here at home!" "Please meet me in the bedroom…I need you to pray, now!"

These were devastating times for us. With all my heart, I believe some of this anguish was spiritual warfare and that Satan viciously attacked me at these moments, taking advantage of my weakness. I would even thrash around feeling out of control. After Greg prayed, the frustration and anger would leave, and weeping would begin. I would sob uncontrollably in my husband's arms feeling demoralized.

I thank God that I have a man who loved me through those agonizing times, telling me that it was okay. He understood, because he had breakdowns as well. His usually took place in his car, with the garage door down, where he thought no one could hear. He yelled at the top of his lungs and cried out in anguish over the unending stress of my condition. My heart ached for him the times that I overheard his own release of pain.

There were other oppressive moments where, out of intense frustration, I would bang my head on the wall or headboard, wanting to hurt myself. Overcome with sorrow, I would scream into a pillow so my family wouldn't hear me.

God did bring about good through all this pain. As a result of these horrible breakdowns, I desperately sought help from the Lord, and it was during this time that He led me to study the "armor of God" in Ephesians 6:10-18. Because of what I learned, I've shared it with others and now place His armor on daily.

Counseling

Licensed professional counselors can be life savers. I encourage you to seek Christian counseling if your circumstances are overwhelming or if you are stuck in a particular stage of grief. There are many gifted, compassionate counselors and pastors who are trained to come along side you and help you process your pain.

My husband and I, and even my children, have benefited from this valuable help. We all needed "talk therapy" at one time or another because of the length and intensity of our trial. God uses counselors in many positive ways and I highly recommend those who approach therapy from a biblical perspective. It is not a sign of weakness, nor shameful to admit that you need help. It is a mark of humility.

I thank God for my dear friend Beth, who lovingly counseled me. I told her about my emotional breakdowns and she empathized with me, understanding the monumental stress I was under. At one point, we talked almost weekly and it helped greatly to have her listen. Over the years, other counselors helped us to recognize when we were not coping in constructive ways. They were gifts sent from God. They each suggested that I find ways to laugh, and we knew it would greatly benefit the whole family...but how?

Laughter

The Bible says *a cheerful heart is a good medicine* (Proverbs 17:22). But to be honest, this did not come easily for me. The physical pain and the depression that followed, along with drug side effects, made laughter impossible at times. One of our friends recommended that we find creative ways to laugh. She suggested that we watch some old "I Love Lucy" and "Andy Griffith" movies to lift the heaviness, and often times this helped.

However, it was primarily my children (and our puppy) that were the biggest source of smiles. Their hugs and jovial ways were a blessed relief. Playing cards and board games with my family has become a positive distraction as well.

Living in the Present

Yet another way to handle a life-threatening condition is to live in the present. "One day at a time," I frequently tell myself. Living in the present has kept me from being bound in fear. This is so important, especially when you have a disease which could turn on you at any given moment. This is a biblical concept as well. When the Israelites were in the desert the Lord fed them manna from heaven each morning. If they stored it away for the next day it spoiled. Only God knows what the future will bring, and He will provide for our needs. Jesus said, *"Therefore do not worry about tomorrow, for tomorrow will worry about itself. Each day has enough trouble of its own."* (Matthew 6:34).

Be Creative

Since I cannot enjoy the sunshine, my husband takes pictures of the kids when they are outdoors doing something fun. Recently when my family went to play miniature golf, Greg knew I would be at my computer, so he emailed pictures from his cell phone. My youngest had never played golf before so in one photo she waved at me. I have to admit, this is bittersweet when viewing pictures of my family taking trips without me. But at least I feel connected in a small way.

I have always wanted to go to the beach with my kids. As I write this, it is summer in South Texas and my family, minus me, will be taking a short trip there. I dread seeing them go because I have wanted so much to experience this with them. We all know that my going along could land me in a hospital, so I will sit at home waiting for more pictures from my husband's cell phone.

I am not going to sit here and tell you that it is easy to watch from the sidelines, by any means. Quite the contrary, being a spectator in the lives of my kids is one of the hardest things I have ever had to do! I will probably be crying as I receive the pictures of them playing in the sand and waves. Nevertheless, I have to trust in the Lord believing that even in the heartbreaking times, His grace is enough.

Dear friends, although there are countless ways to cope, I encourage you to especially treasure the good times when they come. Take pleasure in the little things such as a bubble bath, a butterfly, a flower, a beautiful sunset, a delicious peach, or a simple hug from a friend. Each of these are love letters from the Lord that He does not want us to miss.

What I Learned Lying Down

Chapter 8

Loss, Grief and Acceptance

We all experience loss in this life, and the bigger the loss, the more intense grieving will be. Denial, anger, bargaining, depression and acceptance are all well-known stages of grief, however, grief is individual and complex and does not fit into a neat little package.

Losing my health was like a roller coaster ride with plenty of ups and downs; it was fast and furious until finally, there was acceptance of what God had allowed. There are still tears and sadness at times, but a gentle peace has moved into my heart that says: "God, you know best, and this cross that I bear pleases you. So I surrender sickness, losses, and pain to your perfect will." A dear friend once gave me a poem written by Amy Carmichael titled, "In Acceptance Lieth Peace."[2] I cherished the poem, but it was the title that captured me. The Lord used those four words to speak volumes to me.

But long before that acceptance can take place, we must process pain and loss. This takes time. It took me *only* ten years to come to that place of acceptance, and still I struggle at times because the illness has progressed without remission. An eye-opening moment occurred when my counselor explained that I was experiencing grief over the loss of my health. The thought had never occurred to me. What a comfort that was to hear, because it felt every bit as painful as the grief I experienced over my father's death; different losses yet the same kind of pain. It was also a blessed relief to know I was not crazy!

The losses I experienced due to the disease were gradual, making coping somewhat easier than with sudden loss, but nevertheless grievous. Perhaps the hardest single thing to accept was losing my independence and it still is. I slowly lost my identity I had before becoming sick. Then there was a loss of energy, self-esteem, confidence and friendships. In addition, the disease took away my youth, stamina, strength and the freedom to go out in the sun. Memory loss, bone loss, and hair loss round out the list, and there are still others too personal to share.

Recovery from all of this was near impossible as sorrow rolled over my husband and me like enormous waves. However, the Lord was faithful to comfort us, even on the darkest of days.

May 2007

I am grieving and mourning over so many losses. I ache because it feels I have lost myself. I'm alive and breathing but I have lost sight of what it really feels like to be alive. I catch glimpses of it in other people and I envy it. It hurts. I long to escape the pain, even to run away, but the disease would only follow. Sometimes I hate this sick body because it traps me with all its malfunctions and restrictions. It is so hard to stay positive and I feel like I'm losing my grip and slipping down a steep slope. This week I have felt such deep despair, it has been dreadful and dark. Last night, I just had to get out of the house. I asked Greg to please drive me. I had to leave my children and my visiting mom so I could have a good cry. We did not even make it out of the driveway before big tears filled my eyes. A red cardinal even caught my eye as we left our neighborhood, but it had little effect.

Greg did not know the depth of my despair. I wept in the backseat telling him that I hated my life and wanted to die. He understood where I was at and told me it was okay. His words of validation were exactly what I needed to hear that night. Greg was more than a husband that day. He was an extension of God's hand. He drove me to a nearby lake where there were two benches perched above the water. The sun was setting, but I could not appreciate the beauty because my heart was breaking. For the first time, I wanted to mourn as described in the Old Testament by tearing my clothes and putting ashes over my head as an expression of my grief. In despair, I silently asked the Lord to show me He was near. Minutes later, Greg whispered, "Look Angie, there's a deer." I knew instantly that God sent this creature for me. Her ears were perked up as though she heard me crying. Then we saw her fawn following closely behind. I finally stopped crying as we watched the deer that God sent our way. Sometimes pain is too deep for words. My husband sat with his arm around his deeply broken wife and prayed. I will never forget that night by the lake.

I'm sure some of you can identify with the intense pain I have described. Are you wondering if the pain will ever end? My mom told me once that, "Now is not forever." Those four words were a strange comfort to me at the time. I don't know who said it, but I also like the phrase, "This too shall pass." And thankfully this time of grief did indeed pass. The Bible says, *"Blessed are those who mourn, for they will be comforted"* (Matthew 5:4). Another beautiful verse that comforts me is Psalms 126:5-6:

Those who sow in tears will reap with songs of joy.
He who goes out weeping, carrying seed to sow, will
return with songs of joy, carrying sheaves with him.

I have learned that when you are experiencing a deep loss or multiple losses, you must allow yourself time to grieve. Give yourself permission—it's okay and even cleansing to cry. The shortest verse in the entire Bible is, *"Jesus wept"* (John 11:35). When faced with profound grief or sorrow we can identify with our Savior, sharing in His suffering. *"For we do not have a high priest who is unable to sympathize with our weaknesses, but we have one who has been tempted in every way, just as we are – yet was without sin"* (Hebrews 4:15).

Last night, after I crawled into bed, sadness crept in with me. As I looked back on the weariness of the day the Lord spoke, *"Complete joy cannot come without crosses."* This reminded me of how Jesus endured the cross for the joy set before him (Hebrews 12:2)!

Over time, I learned to focus on gains rather than losses. Dear friend, ask God to show you the good which has come from your loss, even if it's just one thing.

Please understand that I am not attempting to downplay your loss. Grieving is emotionally exhausting and it takes time to recover. Many will never "get over" their loss of a loved one. Some may even get stuck in a particular stage of grief; not knowing the way out. If this is the case, I'd like to reiterate that a compassionate Christian counselor can really help.

As I finish this chapter, my seven year old daughter is sick. She seems to have one health problem after another. In fact, she has medical issues that we have been addressing for a few years. In this mom's opinion, an ailing child is one of the hardest things to watch. At times I find myself thinking, "What if she is going down the same road as me?" With those fearful thoughts, I know I am borrowing trouble from tomorrow, so when I find myself worrying about her little body, I place my Emma in the Lord's hands.

Last night, as she lay weak on the couch recovering from a virus, I told her that God would somehow bring good out of this. She answered, "Mommy, how can there be any good in this?" I explained that maybe we would not see the good here on Earth, but that the Lord is faithful to His promises. He can be trusted, even with our most precious possessions. As my husband carried her off to bed, I hung my hat once again on Romans 8:28.

In our limited minds, we will not always know the good that comes from loss, although I believe God gives us glimpses. Nevertheless, we can know what we don't understand *here* we will know *there!*

In this life you may feel as though you have lost everything, yet you know the love of the Savior, Jesus Christ. If you have placed your hope in him, then dear ones, you have the greatest gain of all.

> *But whatever was to my profit I now consider loss for the sake of Christ. What is more, I consider everything a loss compared to the surpassing greatness of knowing Christ Jesus my Lord, for whose sake I have lost all things. I consider them rubbish that I may gain Christ and be found In Him...*
> (Philippians 3: 7-8)

What I Learned Lying Down

Chapter 9

Fruitful in Affliction

God has made me fruitful in the land of my suffering.
(Genesis 41:52)

Spring has arrived once again and with it comes the reminder that it's pruning time. I love to tend to plants, flowers and for that matter, anything that grows. As my body allows, I've been making rounds to each of the bushes around our house trimming, cutting and shaping. Getting rid of the old growth to make way for the new is something I enjoy.

This past winter, however, I made a fatal mistake with my pruning shears. I used to have a beautiful pink antique rose bush that was fairly close to my kitchen window. It was a profuse bloomer with fragrant pink blossoms nine months out of the year. I loved it! As most gardeners know, you never prune until the danger of a freeze has passed, and untimely pruning was the demise of my favorite rose bush.

For a plant to produce more fruit or flowers it must be cut— and the same is true for us. In John 15:1-2 we read, *"I am the true vine, and my Father is the gardener. He cuts off every branch in me that bears no fruit, while every branch that does bear fruit He prunes so that it will be even more fruitful."* In my case, the Lord did a lot of pruning with the sharp shears of suffering.

One night, while lying in a hospital, I read in Genesis 41:52 that *"God has made me fruitful in the land of my suffering."* That night, the Holy Spirit whispered through His Word telling me that my life would bear fruit even through illness. From that moment on, I knew this was not time wasted. It gave me a sense of purpose knowing that I could be useful to God.

For example, whenever doctor appointments took me away from my children, I reframed the situation by thinking I was on a mission for God. I would load my purse with gospel tracts to hand out to nurses, doctors and staff. Just to tell people that Jesus loved them seemed to lighten their loads, and bring a smile to their faces. In those times I was able to share with patients the real hope that Jesus offers; even when medically, there is no hope. I also brought along Christian magazines, small Bibles, and other books to give out to people as the Lord led. I placed tracts in unusual places like bathroom stalls, praying over them before leaving the restroom. This provided a much needed distraction and it brought me joy in the midst of endless appointments, tests and procedures. For me, it became a way to pass the time with a purpose.

We can trust in the Master Gardener's careful hands as He molds and shapes us, cutting off that which does not bear fruit. The Lord makes no mistakes like I did with my former rose bush. He knows exactly what to allow and what to remove for our continued growth. He wonderfully orchestrates the timing for sun and rain along with the duration needed. Pruning is painful, and frequently it comes in the form of trials, however, your wilderness or desert experience can become a fruitful place where hidden streams in the desert emerge (Isaiah 43:19).

To be fixated on the pain that accompanies a chronic illness is effortless—the challenge lies in looking for the treasures that are hidden in the midst of the pain. For instance, when going in for a dreaded test or procedure, I would ask God to show me something good as a result. Sure, I had my moments where I could see nothing good, but these were more the exception rather than the rule. When you train yourself to think this way, it changes your focus so your eyes are open to riches stored in secret places. It keeps your heart turned upward in thanksgiving as well.

The Lord, our Master, has a divine purpose in affliction and it can be of great benefit to us. The good news is that we can be broken and still bloom. This may sound silly, but I learned this lesson from a geranium! One of its branches had broken almost all the way through. Yet, in the next few days, I noticed that this branch started to blossom. It amazed me that it could still flower under such conditions.

We can be broken and beautiful as well! Our hardships can open doors to share the beautiful love of Christ, as I wrote in this journal entry:

October 2008

Greg and I badly needed a small vacation so we drove a few hours away to a place in the Texas hill country. Traveling takes a huge toll on my body and the next day was spent in bed with swollen joints, chest pain and weakness. I even told my husband that he may have to drive me back home if my condition did not improve. There were feelings of sadness since we both needed the time away together. I knew at best I was going to be cooped up in the room during daylight hours, but at least I would have different walls to look at.

Thankfully, the next morning I was feeling a bit stronger. We slowly walked to the hotel dining room for breakfast. As we met the hostess we told her that we needed a table away from the big windows due to my sun-sensitivity. She looked at us with concern and carefully picked out a table away from the beautiful picture windows. Then she explained to us that her husband had just been diagnosed with cancer and also gets sick with sun exposure. Her burden was heavy. Her eyes looked tired. Her pain was palpable. I glanced at her name tag and we told her that we would be praying for her and her husband. The breakfast was delicious, but my mind kept coming back to Vicki.

As we got up to leave I told Greg that I needed to leave her something. I fumbled through my purse to find a small tract. Quickly, I wrote on the back, "Jesus loves you and He will carry you." She thanked me with tear filled eyes.

Minutes later, as we walked through the hotel we were compelled to stop in the hotel laundry room to pray for her. The next morning we went back to eat breakfast. Vicki looked a little lighter as she seated us again and crouched down by our table to tell us a story that greatly encouraged us. She related how on the morning that I gave her the tract she had prayed for her husband on the way to work. She told God that she needed to know if He had heard her prayers. Just a few short hours after she prayed, we had our encounter. She said that meeting us was her sign that God heard her request. Vicki then shared with us that all five of her adult children had come over to her house that night and she showed them the tract and spoke of what has transpired that day.

God had arranged all these details to come together, not only for Vicki but for her children as well.

Sadly, there have been many opportunities that the Lord presented that I delayed and missed. I'm very glad that I did not let this one slip by. Many in our world are carrying heavy burdens; they are hungry for hope and a word of encouragement.

If we will just take the time we can make a lasting impact in the life of another.

Before leaving for home, I went to tell her good-bye and gave her a letter that the Lord had pressed upon my heart to write the night before. It included verses that had become special to me during the illness. We hugged each other tightly trying to hold back the tears that wanted to fall.

A quiet joy filled me as we drove down the winding road headed for home. I thanked God for the disease that I dislike so much, because had it not been for lupus, I would have never met Vicki. If the sun had not become my enemy, I would have missed the chance to tell her about my friend. You see, many times our loss is heaven's gain. Now, we see through a glass dimly but one day we will see clearly (1 Corinthians 13:12)!

The apostle Paul was fruitful in his afflictions. It was because of an illness that Paul preached the gospel to the Galatians (Galatians 4:13). There is an advantage to being weak because Jesus said that His power is perfected in our weakness (2 Corinthians 12:9). In our infirmities we have the opportunity to experience the power of Christ. Paul even boasted in his afflictions, saying that God's power would rest on him because of it (2 Corinthians 12:9). He took delight in his weakness, insults, hardships, persecutions and difficulties knowing that when he was weak, then he was strong (2 Corinthians 12:10).

Having walked closely with God for almost twenty years, I believe there are some who are teaching and believing in error about illness and healing. Those who are living with disease are fighting a battle that sometimes demands every ounce of strength they have to stay afloat. We need to be very careful about making judgmental remarks to the sick. Often I've heard phrases such as:

"It is not God's will that you be sick." "You could be well if you really wanted to be." "But you don't look sick." I wanted to say, "What does sick look like?" Well-meaning people have said, "You just need to have more faith." I heard all these and more, in subtle and direct ways. I cannot tell you the pain and discouragement it stirs up in the one who is enduring the weight of illness. We start to question and doubt ourselves, as we consider such words, even from friends. Because of these statements the ill start to blame themselves thinking, "it must be our own fault that we are sick." Then guilt creeps in... "*I* am the cause." We start to believe that if we just have more faith then we will be healed. So we muster up all the faith we have and pray for more. We confess every sin we can think of, and ask God to convict us of the ones we may have missed. Then we wait and wait and wait for Jesus to heal us.

God does not heal everyone. Yes, sometimes He chooses to heal, and Praise God for those miracles! Don't misunderstand, I believe wholeheartedly that Jehovah Raphe – the Lord our healer, physically heals today and many of us can testify to His healing power. I'm not trying to discourage you in any way from praying and believing God for great things. Pray for healing in a humble manner.

However, God in His sovereignty doesn't always choose to remove our disease or disability. When Paul asked three times for his thorn to be removed, the Lord responded by saying that His grace would be sufficient for him (2 Corinthians 12:9).

How encouraging and inspiring it has been to read stories of those who have had a powerful impact on the kingdom of God and yet were afflicted, whether with disease, disability or handicap.

Here are just a few examples of phenomenal Christian heroes that have been fruitful, and at the same time afflicted: Charles Spurgeon, Abraham Lincoln, Amy Carmichael, Billy Graham, Fanny Crosby, Bill Bright and Joni Erickson Tada. Did these great saints have little faith? I think not. Did they have some secret sins that were not confessed? I don't believe so. These great men and women were made stronger by their afflictions, and the power of Christ was and is evident in their lives.

Charles Spurgeon (1834-1892) was a well known preacher to a flock of 10,000. Known as "the prince of preachers", he wrote sermons and weekly newspaper columns. He also tended to orphans. It is said of him that he limped to the pulpit, sometimes having to kneel on one knee for stability. This godly servant suffered from depression, debilitating gout and Bright's disease (chronic kidney inflammation). From the age of thirty-five he was afflicted with one illness after another until his death at age 57.

Abraham Lincoln, the 16th president of the United States, suffered from depression, and nearly died from smallpox. It has been said that he was in the early stages of the disease when he gave one of the most well known speeches of all time, "The Gettysburg Address." His life was then cut short by an assassin's bullet.

Amy Carmichael, pioneer missionary to India during the late 1800's, took in hundreds of orphans and founded the Dohnavur Fellowship. She was a teacher and mentor, bringing many of India's forgotten children to faith in Jesus Christ. For twenty years, she suffered from neuralgia that made her so weak that she was bedridden for weeks on end. It was during this time she penned many of her inspiring books and beautiful poems.

Billy Graham, one of the most famous evangelists of the twentieth century, suffers from Parkinson's disease, prostate cancer and has had a shunt to drain fluid off his brain from hydrocephalus. Fruit produced? Countless thousands whose lives have been changed through this man who has completely surrendered to the Lord.

Fanny Crosby, author of 8,000 poems and hymns, was blinded at birth due to a mistake made by her doctor. Songs such as "To God Be the Glory" and "Blessed Assurance" testify of the fruit she bore through suffering.

Bill Bright, the founder of Campus Crusade for Christ and the producer of the well known "Jesus film" fought diabetes and lived on oxygen for the last few years of his life due to pulmonary fibrosis. The fruit? Millions of lives saved through the Film translated into 1,050 languages! This film is said to be one of the greatest evangelistic tools of all time.

Joni Erickson Tada, famous Christian author and speaker, injured her spine in a diving accident as a teenager, paralyzing her from the neck down. She writes, speaks, sings, and even draws with her teeth all for the glory of God! She has a foundation that ministers to the disabled and raises funds for wheelchairs. Joni has become an inspiration to millions, including me.

The Bible has much to say about suffering. *"For it has been granted to you on behalf of Christ not only to believe on him, but also to suffer for him."* (Philippians 1:29). Jesus himself suffered unbelievable agony as He was nailed to a cross for us. The Apostle Paul said that, *"We must go through many hardships to enter the kingdom of God"* (Acts 14:22). Many of God's servants written about in the Bible were allowed by their heavenly Father to experience intense trials and suffering. We need to look no further than Job.

What if there was no book of Job? Then comfort, wisdom and truth gained from these pages would be lost. I doubt Job knew that his story would be the eighteenth book of the Bible, and that it would be read by millions of weary sojourners. I have been comforted through this gripping story time and time again. If you are suffering, and have not read the book of Job, I encourage you to read this amazing book which teaches us about the sovereignty of God through His suffering servant.

Praise be to the God and Father of our Lord Jesus Christ, the Father of compassion and the God of all comfort, who comforts us in all our troubles, so that we can comfort those in any trouble with the comfort we ourselves have received from God. For just as the sufferings of Christ flow over into our lives, so also through Christ our comfort overflows. (2 Corinthians 1:3-5)

What I Learned Lying Down

Chapter 10

In Sickness and In Health

...I found him whom my soul loves...
(Song of Solomon 3:4 NASB)

My husband Greg and I have been married for fifteen years; twelve of those fifteen I have been sick, to one degree or another. I'm so thankful that God chose him to weather these storms with me. The Lord knew that I needed someone to stay by my side as the seas would get very rough. He is my hero and has become my best friend, but unfortunately, Greg has had to learn to wear many hats—ones I know he did not expect he would ever have to wear. But that is what defines our commitment; taking our vows seriously, even though there have been times when we wanted to run.

He has become a strong prayer warrior, for etched in my memory are many nights that he knelt beside my bed crying out to God, while I lay weak and in pain, or struggling to breathe. He's my companion, counselor, nurse, protector, chauffer, shoulder to cry on, and caregiver. When my memory fails me, I look to him so my other, much smarter, brain can take over. He has been my defender as well, challenging the doctors when they put me on trial.

There were months when I was too weak to walk. He then became my legs, pushing me in a wheelchair. I think he actually liked that part the most, especially if we were in a shopping mall. As I pointed to something in the store window, he just kept pushing; acting as though he could not hear me.

During the many times I was hospitalized, my husband smuggled in special meals from favorite restaurants, and often arrived with chocolate, new pajamas, slippers, socks or flowers. I readily admit that I've been spoiled. In addition to taking care of me, he had to be daddy to our three precious children and hold down a full-time job.

Frequently, he had to be mommy too. I grieved over the mommy duties that he had to take over. Guilt threatened to drag me into a downward spiral because I desperately wanted to be his helper. He tried so hard to fill in the gap for me, but still I ached for what I was unable to do for him and the children.

Numerous mornings he got the children ready for school while I slept. I'm sure the teachers knew the days I could not get out of bed because of the girls' mismatched clothes, and undone hair. I tried to give Greg ponytail lessons, but he never seemed to catch on. There are some things only a mom can do! Most mornings, he fed them breakfast and I kissed the children goodbye from bed. He rarely missed a field trip and did all the grocery shopping and cooking when I could not.

I love the fact that the Lord knows what we need before we ask, and He knew in advance that I would need a husband with the gift of serving. Needless to say, Greg was often exhausted so whenever I had an occasional break from the pain and weakness, I served him gladly. Undoubtedly God has given him supernatural strength, and amazing grace to stand up under a very heavy load.

It should go without saying that we both felt despair and anguish on many occasions. At times we felt as if our marriage was being ripped apart. In all honesty, I envied Greg's health and his freedom. He took the kids out for summer activities while I was left home alone. On one hand, I felt happy that they were out for a fun day. On the other hand, I was sad that I was constantly a bystander. Yes, I smiled at the kids and blew them kisses; I told them to have fun, and really meant it, but as the garage door hit the hard floor— so would I.

Each time they left, I was once again locked in my prison (our home) only to weep for the freedom I had lost. Loneliness would descend like a heavy blanket around me. One of the hardest parts of chronic illness is loneliness. Isolation aches like nothing else. Until one has walked a mile in your shoes they can't truly understand what you face each day, but Jesus does understand and He has a purpose in the pain. It was during the loneliest times that I felt God ushering me into a deeper walk with Him.

Jesus wanted me to sit still at His feet; to cease striving and really know Him (Psalm 46:10 NASB). I was not alone as the Lord was present in my sorrow, teaching me to reframe my pain in a fresh new light. It was about being content in whatsoever state I was in (Philippians 4:11 KJV). This meant that even if I was unable to go outside until dusk, the Lord wanted me to be content. This is a very hard pill to swallow, yet one that I knew God was calling me to. Contentment is not something learned overnight, but over years. God taught me contentment in the circumstances that surrounded me, and this brought me peace as I continued to walk in the rain.

Throughout this illness, I have learned that sometimes pain is too deep for words. In these moments, there is nothing the caregiver can do, but just be with the sick one. Greg is a "fixer" like most men, and it absolutely unnerved him that he could not "fix" me. For instance, when I was in pain, he wanted to know what pill to get, when all I wanted was for him to sit beside me and hold my hand. There was no quick fix, even though we yearned for one.

Of course there is time for action, but there is also time to be still. This goes against our nature because we want to *do* something for the one we love. Truly, the times that I could just lie still in my husband's arms were of great comfort to me.

The never ending challenges surrounding chronic illness can change the dynamics of a marriage. Our marriage wasn't the same as it once was, but then, very little stays the same. Jesus is the only one who is the same yesterday, today and forever (Hebrews 13:8).

Unfortunately, I became so dependent on my husband that frankly, I began to resent his "control" over me. From his point of view he was trying to protect me, but I felt smothered. Please don't misunderstand me, I am so blessed to have a husband that loves and cares for me. One thing is certain, if God had not been the glue holding our marriage together, we would not have made it. Greg eventually realized that he had to rely on the Grand Fixer, Jesus Christ, and place his full trust in the one who created us.

Along with loneliness, guilt is another obstacle for the chronically ill. I'm not referring to the remorse we feel when we are convicted of sin, but a false guilt. I would go so far as to say that it is one of our enemies. False guilt is from our adversary, who wants to use it to steal our joy and destroy us. Guilt has certainly been one of the more difficult issues for me, and still I wrestle with it occasionally. It would inevitably sneak in as I watched Greg doing "mommy chores" while I lay on the couch.

When my husband stressed over all the tasks he had to juggle, self-condemnation took root. Only by praying God's Word constantly, has this stronghold been broken, Praise God!

So many of my responsibilities now rested on his shoulders, that I felt like such a burden to him, although he always assured me that I was not. Still, it was hard to shake the thought that I was a millstone hung around his neck, dragging him and the children down. I now know that this thought was not my own, but one that Satan planted in my mind.

As intensely as Greg loved and served, he also found himself at times depressed, resentful and even angry— common emotions for worn out caregivers. As long as the anger was not directed at me, it was understandable. But as resentment built, he started unleashing it on me. Sometimes his pain came out in harsh words that cut deeply.

Greg was grieving over the many losses he incurred because of the disease. We tried to find ways to vent our frustration. We even discussed buying some cheap dishes and breaking them on the garage floor, or setting up a punching bag to release tension. Some of you who are going through chronic illness with a spouse fully understand the frustration that builds up on both sides.

To my husband's credit, I was a difficult patient at times. When the amount of steroids prescribed was increased, my mood went south, and I even picked fights with him. Furthermore, I became extremely irritable; taking out my frustration on Greg (this was very out of character for me). Those of you who have been on steroids for a long time understand what I'm talking about. They are bittersweet. These drugs help put out the fire, but leave you cantankerous along with a host of other side effects.

Feeling sick most of the time caused me to complain too much, and unfortunately, Greg was my sounding board. Not only did I wear out his ears unloading all my hurts, but it seemed that late nights were prime time for me to unload my dump truck. Poor Greg, this was the time that he needed his sleep.

Now it makes sense to me, that anxiety and anger developed. I am not saying that his outbursts were justified, because they can be very damaging to a relationship, and I know he would agree. Greg said many times he wished he could punch the disease. I completely understood, except, it resided in me. And as a result of tremendous, unending stress, I became the verbal "punching bag" so to speak (this was never physical). This usually happened during my weakest times, which left deep wounds in my heart. Consequently, I built strong walls around my heart to protect it from further hurt.

Several times he drove off in frustration and I did not know if, or when he would return. Nevertheless, I understood why Greg needed to escape. I wanted to run too! But alas, the disease would only follow. Experiences like these shattered my self esteem, leaving me scarred, vulnerable and feeling even more alone. I would go to my knees by the front window of our home weeping, praying and waiting for God to bring him home. I felt insecure during these times because of the failed relationship in my past. This is an example of one of our many difficult days and how God provided for and met our needs:

June 2004

Our marriage has been severely stressed due to this unrelenting disease. To make matters worse, the doctor placed me on high dose steroids which make me very irritable. Speaking from one who has been on steroids for years, one of the side effects is that you grow lovely facial hair (I did not want sideburns, thank you)! They also can add extra pounds, change the shape of your face, and give you the appetite of a horse. The only sweet side to this bitter pill is that painful inflammation is reduced.

Our special friends from Round Rock told us they would like to come for a visit. They are a few years older than us and have enjoyed our kids as "grandchildren." It was a no-brainer when they asked if they could take the kids off our hands for a few hours to give us some time alone. It sounded good at the time, but shortly after they all left, Greg and I broke out into a fight. I'm feeling so smothered by him lately! He is constantly asking me if I took this pill or that. So I decided to go out to my small flower garden for some time alone. To my dismay, out walked Greg to talk to me. I ended up shutting down, giving him the silent treatment. (I have learned that this is not the way to handle conflict.) Greg got so angry at me for shutting down that he picked up the pitcher I was using to water my plants with, and threw it up against the brick wall. Plastic flew everywhere. He then felt bad about breaking the pitcher so he went into the garage to find another one. He gave it to me, and I made an unkind remark so he took that one and threw it too! At least he got his frustration out. I just sat there numb.

The night was not going well at all, and I knew our friends would be returning soon with the children. Greg then decided to get on his bike and said, "See ya!" Oh, I could have killed him...He was mad and so was I! At least I knew he couldn't get very far on that bike. I came inside the house and began thinking, "Here are our dear friends, he is a Baptist deacon, and she is a professional counselor. They have come for a visit and we haven't seen them in months. Greg is mad at me out on his bike somewhere?! And I look like something the cat drug in." He finally came back from his bike ride, and found me sitting in our toddler's room in the rocking chair. I thought, "Oh no – Please leave me alone." He began to tell me to push through the steroid side-effects. I shouted, "GREG...I am trying!" All the while I am looking at this toy stick horse in the corner of the room. The horse started to look very tempting because of the long, hard, wooden stick on the end. I told him that if he told me to break through the side-effects one more time, that I was going to break him with that stick horse! We both began to laugh...thank goodness, and some tension was lifted.

Greg asked me to forgive him for his anger and I apologized too. This happened not a moment too soon because minutes later our friends walked in the door with the kids in tow. These friends are very special ministers to our family, and we would not have made it through this trial without them. She offered to give the girls a bath for me. Thank you Jesus! Oh, how we desperately needed them that night. He came over to the couch where I was sitting, and covered my legs with a blanket, giving me a hug. His act of kindness was all it took for me to start crying. I could not let go of his neck. Charles patted my head and knelt down and prayed for me. These wonderful friends had no idea what they were walking into that night, but God knew that we would need them. They were Jesus to us that night. Beth ministered to us both by giving us a marathon counseling session until midnight. How we needed it! God used them both as a team, and when they left Greg and I walked inside holding hands.

It was during these broken times when we saw God's love in action through his servants. This is just one example of many. It was also during these times that God instructed me to pray for my husband night and day. I was to make my husband my primary prayer priority. I learned through watching him struggle that he needed me to intercede and pray for him in all areas of his life. "The Power of a Praying Wife" by Stormie

O'Martian, was a tool that the Lord used to teach me about praying for my husband. We know our husbands better than anyone else. Especially during these evil days, they have struggles and temptations bombarding them from all sides. Who better to pray for them daily than their wives? We then get a front row seat to watch God work His miracles through our prayers.

In addition to our prayers, husbands need our respect. The Bible clearly says that the wife must respect her husband (Ephesians 5:33). It is also written, *"Wives submit to your husbands as to the Lord"* (Ephesians 5:22). I have failed miserably with these commands at times. I was not pleasing God when I showed disrespect toward my husband, though it has always been my desire to please the Lord. I rationalized my attitude because of his temper and outbursts, but I learned that God wanted me to give Greg unconditional respect regardless of his actions. The bottom line is that God has called wives to respect their husbands. Just as women must know that they are loved, men need our respect like they need air to breathe. We must build our husbands up by speaking words of life to them.

One of the first healing steps took place when I got on my face and asked God's forgiveness for the resentment that I had harbored against my husband because of his anger. A weight was instantly lifted and walls began to come down. It was amazing! Resentment can create a huge wedge, dividing two people, and in addition, it is sin.

It may help those with troubled marriages for me to share that Greg and I thought that our broken marriage was beyond repair. We did not even sleep in the same bedroom for a year. I thought our love had died. We could not see how this marriage could possibly recover, apart from a miracle. Our relationship was broken, but not beyond repair. When we find ourselves in a dark trial, it seems that the sun will never shine again, but is anything too hard for the Lord? (Genesis 18:14). If God can restore our marriage, without a doubt He can restore yours. In fact, He wants nothing more than to do that for you. Jesus can heal the deepest wounds to our hearts and rekindle love that we think is long gone. He still performs miracles every day. My marriage is living proof of that!

Today, we are still unable to make plans until the last minute, and we never know what tomorrow may bring, but we have learned complete dependence on God. We live one day at a time. I still have to push guilt away on occasion for not being able to be everything a healthy wife can be. Even so, we give thanks to God for how he has delivered our marriage from misery to joy, and we pray that it will be a testimony that glorifies and honors our Lord.

If your marriage relationship is hanging by a thread, I encourage you to persevere through the trial. DON'T GIVE UP! Hold on. It is well worth it. With Jesus as Lord of your life, you can make it through absolutely anything. Remember, *"...with God all things are possible"* (Matthew 19:26). I sit here today with a stronger marriage than ever before; a marriage that nothing but death can separate. I'll never doubt that Greg was handpicked by God to love me in sickness and in health, and he has done just that. Our marriage is not perfect but it is healthy. We pray that our story will give you renewed hope to press on. Your children will thank you, as well as your grandchildren.

Chapter 11

Mommy from the Couch

I can do all things through him who strengthens me.
(Philippians 4:13 NASB)

"Mommy, do you sometimes feel like you are hanging onto monkey bars?"

"Yes," I said to my daughter Mary (who was nine at the time).

She continued, "Well, God is proud of you for holding on." I held back the tears as I sipped my soup, cherishing every single word she had just said. She turned around and continued eating her peanut butter and jelly sandwich, unaware of how God had used her.

The Lord has richly blessed me with three precious children. God, in his wisdom, knew just how much I would need them, and how much they would need me. I truly believe had it not been for these gifts, I would have given up on this battle long ago. They are my comforters, my prayer warriors and my joy, often cheering me on and encouraging me not to give up or lose hope. I'm in awe of how the Lord has spoken treasures of truth through them, at the precise moments I have encountered discouragement and pain. They are His instruments, as I had prayed they would be.

I'm reminded of when my youngest child, Emma, was five years old, and had a terrible case of bacterial pneumonia.

For the first time, I truly thought that I might lose a child and I was an emotional wreck. After a second x-ray, the doctor phoned to tell me that the pneumonia was worse than suspected and that the mass in her lung was now solid. I remember the nausea that swept over me as I thought about the foreign mass in her small lung.

When I got off the telephone I went to her room to lie down with her. Emma's little body had become weak, her color was poor and she had missed more than a month of kindergarten. As I watched my baby sleeping, staring at her angelic face, she stirred a little and with eyes still closed took her thumb out of her mouth and said, *"Nothing is a giant to God."* The thumb went back in and she fell asleep. I was blown away! God saw my concern and was giving me *exactly* what I needed at just the right time. A few days later as they x-rayed her chest, the mass was gone! Our doctor said pneumonia of this type does not just disappear. She said we had all witnessed a miracle.

Since I was not well, there were days I would look at my children and feel sadness that they could not participate in activities like other kids. Planning a birthday party for my children was something that I rarely had the strength to do. Although they asked many times, things like baseball for my son or ballet for the girls were not possible because of my poor health. Success to us was getting them to school each weekday and church on Sunday mornings. Once, when I was very sick lying down, I whispered to myself with tears, "My poor kids." The Lord spoke, *"They are rich in every way, and I am teaching my truths to them through this trial."* It was also during these times that the Lord would remind me again of Romans 8:28: (KJV)

And we know that all things work together for good to them that love God, to them who are the called according to his purpose.

When I could not figure out the chaos that was unfolding in my body, I held tight to this promise. God had allowed this illness for His Glory, and He knew well in advance that my children would have a sick mother. Somehow, it all fit into His perfect plan. Over and over I would have to trust God. He would bring good through this illness in my life, and to the lives of my family. This disease had not caught my heavenly Father by surprise, for he loved Matthew, Mary and Emma much more than I ever could. I sometimes wondered why God gave me these wonderful kids if I was going to be sick all their lives. But I didn't have to look very far to see the spiritual gifts He was blessing them with.

I will never forget the summer my son was eight years old. I was trying to wash the dishes one morning, when he looked up at me and calmly asked if he could have a pulpit for his birthday. Stunned, I looked out the kitchen window and said, "We'll see honey," as I wondered how in the world I was going to deliver on this request? Once he walked away, I knew this was no ordinary moment, but then Matthew was no ordinary child. He began reading his Bible at age four. His children's Bible wouldn't do, so he asked to read mine. When he was six he started "preaching." He would set up "church" in our large foyer, propping up stuffed animals in every chair he could find. He would then insist that Mary lead the singing. Emma, then two, would sit on the front row in her rocking chair. Her thumb would be firmly inserted in her mouth while "Bubby" as his sisters called him, preached into his Little Tike's microphone. The landing of our staircase served as his platform. And Matthew would call the girls down if they were not paying attention - it was priceless!

Now twelve, his sermons have matured and he seems to have the gift of preaching. By the way, God delivered on the pulpit request. I mentioned this to a friend, and little did I know, she told her husband who felt impressed to build him a beautiful pulpit. It stands in our living room today as a reminder to me of Psalm 37:4: *"Delight yourself in the LORD and he will give you the desires of your heart."*

I believe God is delighted with Matthew as he gives sermons to adults now, and no longer to his fuzzy friends. He types them on the computer giving each one a catchy title. My husband and I are always lifted up as our girls sing songs, and our son prays for our family, speaking timely words into our weary hearts. As babies we fed them and now they feed us.

Our girls have been tremendous blessings as they are little nurses and encouragers. I see gifts of mercy and encouragement that the Lord is instilling in my young daughters. Their tender comfort, beautiful handmade cards, and endless hugs have been precious gifts. I have drawings of me in a bed looking pretty with a smile across my face, when in reality that was far from the case. One memory I treasure is how they both would offer their favorite bear and blanket to comfort me. Whenever I was struggling, Mary would take my face in her hands telling me that one day God was going to heal me. Even now as I write, Emma has been bringing me pictures of her mommy healed.

I was especially touched when my children would come to my bedside or "couch side" and say, "Mommy, do you want me to pray for you?" God would tap me on the shoulder and say, *"You see... I am teaching them to pray."* Countless times we had no other way out of the situation or pain we were in.

We couldn't go to the emergency room every time I was in a crisis. No, God wanted our family of five to completely depend on Him, so as a result we turned to prayer often. I guess you could say that my kids grew up on their knees.

Still, I couldn't be the mom I wanted to be. One day my next door neighbor, who was in her mid-seventies, came over and played baseball with my son. She was agile having played sports most of her life. At only thirty-eight, I felt like I was one hundred years old as I watched sadly from the couch inside. I remain very grateful for those who give of their time to do activities with my children, such as taking them swimming, to the park, to the zoo or shopping. But it was heartbreaking to watch people twice my age run circles around me, and do the things that I longed to do.

Sometimes, I wanted someone to put a paper bag over my head so my husband and children would not have to look on my misery. I would see the hurt in their eyes and try to give them my best, weak smile, while I was crying on the inside. I longed to give them more of myself– to go on bike rides, to chase them around the backyard, kick the ball and run with them, or take them to the beach. I missed the simple things that a healthy mother takes for granted, like grocery shopping and field trips. It was during those moments I had to ask God for His eyes, so I could see this all from His eternal perspective. I would fall into self-pity if I didn't meditate on the truth of God's words constantly. Comfort and peace came as I redirected my thoughts. The Lord wanted me to fix my eyes yet again on Him and not my circumstances.

So we fix our eyes not on what is seen, but on what is unseen. For what is seen is temporary, but what is unseen is eternal. (2 Corinthians 4:18)

I was "Mommy from the couch"; directing homework, reading stories and playing games while curled up in a blanket. I taught them lessons about the Lord as He was teaching them to me. I've come to learn that we can't teach our children to be still and know that He is God if we are always on the run. The Lord gave me no choice in the matter. I was not able to go to and fro and He wanted it that way. For this reason, our family was forced to spend tremendous amounts of "downtime" together.

We can see clearly now that God has given us an unexpected gift (though it did not seem like a gift at the time). He pulled our family off the merry-go-round of "normal" life to set us aside while everyone around us buzzed with activity. This seemed like such a loss, but now I see that it has been to our gain. I feel like God taught us in His way, the secret of a quiet, simple life. As a result, we have had many precious hours with our children really getting to know them, and we are constantly reaping the benefits.

Parents, our children need us like never before. Time is one of the best gifts we can give to our sons and daughters especially while they are young and impressionable. We must be careful to carve out time for them, because if we don't the world will. Everything calls for our attention, while our kids desperately try to get ours. It seems like our society is moving at warp speed and families are more stressed than ever. Our bodies are not designed for this fast pace, and neither are our children.

Since I couldn't go with my feet, I had to do something. I was driven to make my time count for Christ. I would think, "What if I don't have many years left with my children?" Of course, none of us has any guarantee that we have tomorrow.

So my focus became their spiritual health. Our kids need to be equipped with God's Word in this dark world they are growing up in. If Jesus tarries, I'm afraid that my children will one day face persecution because of their faith. Our soldiers need to be prepared for the battlefield. We cannot rely on the church to do this; it is our duty, or may I say privilege, as parents. Therefore, I desperately yearn for them to know Jesus in a real and personal way. This actually began by sharing with them one of my passions.

As soon as my children could read I encouraged them to read their Bibles daily.

I love God's Word and wanted to share this love with them, so I explained to them that the Bible is like a treasure chest. I would ask my children almost daily "Did you get your treasure?" They liked this analogy, and did not want to miss their treasure.

Pouring God's Word into these young hearts, I found that I was learning many truths as well. Isn't it humbling how we teach our kids a Bible story or lesson and God uses is to hit us right between the eyes? I wonder if God may be showing us His sense of humor during these moments when we think we are training our children, but in reality, God is training us through them. They led me many times and grew my faith...this brings to mind an insightful verse in the Old Testament: *"...and a little child will lead them"* (Isaiah 11:6).

It has been said that God wraps up blessings in disguise. Now, I can plainly see that this illness has really been a gift wrapped in unattractive paper. I'm truly thankful for what the Lord has allowed, and for what I have learned about parenting as a mommy from the couch.

Fix these words of mine in your hearts and minds; tie them as symbols on your hands and bind them on your foreheads. Teach them to your children, talking about them when you sit at home and when you walk along the road, when you lie down and you get up. (Deuteronomy 11:18-19)

Chapter 12

Miracles in New Mexico

The burden of suffering seems a tombstone hung about our necks, while in reality it is only the weight which is necessary to keep down the diver while he is hunting for pearls. [3] – Jean Paul Richter

By the summer of 2005, we were desperate for help. My rheumatologist said there was nothing more he could do. These were very difficult words to hear. I was strapped to an oxygen machine much of the time and sicker than ever. We had reason to believe, from recent pulmonary tests, that my lungs had now become a target of the lupus. This was bad news, and to make matters worse, I could not tolerate the strong medicines that are typically used to slow down the disease. Medically speaking, the only option I had was symptom control and pain management.

It was at this time that Dr. John, my gastroenterologist, recommended that we take a trip out west to see if the climate and better air quality would benefit my health. At this point, we would have gone to Timbuktu if we were given some hope of healing, or even just a better quality of life.

This trip made no practical sense because of my precarious condition. But we covered the decision in prayer, and asked many others to pray as well. In just a short time, we felt God directing us to go, and it seemed all lights were green.

This in turn gave me hope that maybe I would feel better in the mountains. Dr. John even gave me the name and phone number of one of his patients that had moved to a little mountain town in southern New Mexico and improved. After our conversation, my hope soared!

But just a few days before we were to leave, I almost passed out in church. Our pastor helped Greg carry me to the car that Sunday (not the first time that I've been carried out of a church by the pastor). Now we felt apprehensive. One thing was certain; this adventure was going to require a huge leap of faith. At least we knew that the Lord would be our guide.

The following is based on journal entries: July 11–18, 2005

DAY 1

Today we are leaving for New Mexico. Greg and I are flying west to see if my health improves. We have hope that it will, because several of Dr. John's patients have benefited from living in a higher elevation, away from the gulf coast, chemical plants and pollution. Our pastor and his wife were so kind to take us to the airport. Greg insisted that he push me in a wheelchair through the airport. Because of the near fainting episodes last week I knew I needed to let him do this. Still, it is very hard to accept, that at age 36, I need a wheelchair for long distances.

As we exited the plane, I was thankful for my seat with wheels because the airport was quite large. When we arrived, the temperature was a blazing 102 degrees. Fatigue and irritability were setting in as I was wearing out. We got the rental car and set out for Cloudcroft, about two hours north. It was a steady climb, and we watched as the scenery changed quickly from desert to mountains. The closer we got to our final destination, the more breathtaking the landscape was.

The sun was setting as we pulled into the lodge where we had reserved a room. I stepped out of the car and marveled at the beauty before me. The hotel was perched high on a peak, looking out over a forested mountain range. The surroundings were cool and crisp, serene and picturesque. What a stark contrast from the smog, humidity and noise of Houston we left just hours earlier. Words fail me, because there are none to describe this moment in my life. The moon in the sky was as bright as it could be, and a shining star caught my eye, as the sun slowly set in the west. My parents had been to Cloudcroft several times on getaways, and now I could understand why they loved this place.

There was a small pond with a beautiful fountain in front of the lodge complete with various floral displays. It was at that moment, I was completely overwhelmed with the presence of God. Tears streamed down my cheeks because the Lord was so near and I felt that maybe my daddy in heaven was peering down, looking at his daughter.

The gorgeous view alone was well worth the trip – exhaustion and all. We ate a light dinner in the hotel dining room looking out the picture windows, while a pianist played "Morning Has Broken." It was a feast for the eyes, ears and taste buds. Even though my pain was starting to escalate, it felt like I had been transported to another place and time.

After the lovely meal, we drove to our cabin. We were worn out, but surprised that so far, I did not need the oxygen that I had been requiring for weeks back home. However, after being in our room only a short time, I started to get congested. I blew it off thinking it was my allergies. An hour or so later, what started off as an ache in my chest began to grow worse. Our concern turned to worry when my legs became very weak, along with other strange symptoms.

In desperation, I placed a call to Jean, the patient of Doctor John's that I had contacted before leaving Houston. A few years prior, she and her husband had moved here to Cloudcroft from the Houston area. She prayed with me, and my spirit was calmed. "Thank you, God, for the body of Christ"

DAY 2

My second day in Cloudcroft is not starting off well. My head is killing me, my nose stuffy, and my chest aches. Greg got breakfast for us, and after we ate he went exploring the little town by himself. In the meantime, I was left wondering why my head was pounding. The old room smelled of mildew and mold. We found out later that the cabin had been built over one-hundred years ago and was used for skiers. That explained the worn out indoor/outdoor carpet and the mildew. I told Greg I needed to get out of the room. We took a drive and ended up going to see where my new friend Jean lived. Strangely, I started to feel better the further we got from the room.

We drove up to Jean and Bob's house. What a precious godly couple they were; I am in awe of how God arranged our meeting. We walked upstairs, however, by this time my body had weakened significantly. Breathless, I was so glad to be able to sit down on their front porch, which was on the second floor of the house set among the trees. It was one of the most tranquil settings I have ever seen. During the summer, the hummingbirds migrate to the area. I have never seen so many hummingbirds in all my life! Greg and I were fascinated by them, and the sound of their wings buzzing, reminded me of a mini airport. These little speedy wonders were mesmerizing. The porch was a beautiful retreat. The fir, pine, and aspen trees surrounding us were gorgeous, and I loved the crisp mountain air. It felt like a bit of heaven sitting on top of this mountain.

I still did not feel well, but was enjoying talking to this new friend, who had been seriously ill for so many years. She was like a shot of hope to me, because she looked like a picture of health now. She and her husband were very encouraging to us both, but as we talked, I was physically sinking...and fast. My blood pressure was low and when we got up to leave I almost blacked out. Bob was so kind; he was on one side and Greg on the other, trying to get me down the many steps to our car. I had to stop however, to sit down and I asked them to pray for me. After their prayer, I continued to walk with assistance feeling like I was eighty years old.

We finally made it down to the car, and Jean picked some wild daisies, handing them to me. We then slowly drove away to find a place to turn around and head down the hill. Where we had to turn around we were amused to read a sign before us that read: "Malfunction Junction." How ironic! I felt this is where I was in my journey as well. It was a rustic, wooden sign, with the words engraved in white. We both were astonished with this peculiar sign. So much so that I just had to take a picture of it, which is still on my refrigerator today. At least it made us both laugh, something we needed. On the return trip to our musty cabin, I felt a bit anxious, so I focused on the beautiful landscape.

Not long after we got back into the cabin, my symptoms started to worsen. My head began to ache, my chest hurt, and my eyes grew very heavy. Something in the room was affecting me terribly. Greg was extremely frustrated and angry, while I became irritable. He said in a stern tone, "Angie...I cannot believe I let you talk me into bringing you to New Mexico! What on earth was I thinking?" Very upset, I called my dear friend Cindi, back in Houston to pray for us.

After her prayer, I was comforted, so I decided to walk out of the room and sit on the porch. I told Greg we were going to have to stay somewhere else. He asked me if I thought I could travel about one hour to Ruidoso, since there were no other places to stay in this little town. With the chest pain increasing I didn't see how I could travel anywhere very far. Being in a faraway place, and not knowing what to do, we called on our new friends, the Bolton's, again. After hearing our desperate situation, they said they could move their trailer to a nearby RV park for us to use. We were so appreciative, yet alarmed that this was even happening on the second day of our trip.

Bob showed us the very nice RV, but understandably Greg insisted I walk inside and smell it, before he would have Bob move it. He was so frustrated with me, and my body's weird reactions, but I could not help what was happening. I began to feel more and more pain in my chest, especially around the heart. It reminded me of the time when I had pericarditis. We decided to accept the gracious offer of the RV, but I was in misery by this time. As we drove to the RV park just outside of town, I clutched a pillow over my chest just trying to bear up a little longer.

We followed Mr. Bolton who was pulling the trailer to the RV park—we had just met him for the very first time today, and now he was providing us with a clean place to rest! His wife Jean rode with us, telling us that the owners of the park were Christians and attended their church. When we arrived, they immediately began to help. I watched from the back seat of the car, as these strangers began to help us settle in; unloading the car and setting up the trailer. In the meantime, oxygen was helping a little, but the pain was very intense causing me to worry. I should mention the fact that I even had oxygen for the trip was a miracle. Since the airline could not allow me to carry oxygen, the Lord had provided yet another Christian couple near the airport in El Paso who had arranged for us to have a supply when we landed.

So I began to pray, "God please help me! Sustain me. I am in trouble. Lord, I know you did not bring me out here to die. Please have mercy Lord."

The next thing I knew there were six people around me trying to help me to the bed inside the RV, (one of them was a trained paramedic). By this time, I could barely walk, and their help was a godsend. The park owners along with many other campers were lending a hand. God provides in amazing ways for his children. Jean and another sweet lady, Mary Alice, helped me to bed with oxygen attached while Greg had to drive back into town to retrieve our luggage. Mary Alice went to her trailer to get vegetable soup for me and Jean said she would feed it to me if I was too weak to hold a spoon. As I told these sisters in Christ about my journey, my faith increased. He was using His own to take care of us in a time of need – and they were everywhere! I slept with oxygen that night and rested in bed most of the next day. The following morning, these kind hearted people from the RV park served us by bringing all kinds of food.

...I tell you the truth, whatever you did for the least of these brothers and sisters of mine, you did for me (Matthew 25:40).

DAY 3

Today is not much better, but I'm waiting for things to turn around. I'm still short of breath with stinging pain across my chest. Again I prayed:

"Lord, what are you up to? I felt strongly that you wanted us to come to New Mexico. With child-like faith I will trust you to guide us along this uncharted path."

For I know the plans I have for you," declares the LORD, "plans to prosper you and not to harm you, plans to give you hope and a future. Then you will call upon me and come and pray to me, and I will listen to you. You will seek me and find me when you seek me with all your heart. (Jeremiah 29:11-13)

This really encourages me because I know from this passage that God listens when we call upon His name. I'm anxious about getting on a plane in just two days to go home. It nearly killed me to get out here, and right now I don't know how I will travel home. "Jesus, help me to seek you with all my heart and trust in your plan."

DAY 4

Well, my plan was to rest all day in Cloudcroft, but God had something else in mind. I rested in the morning and we went back to the Bolton's home in the late afternoon. I am slow and extremely weak today. So weak that Bob and Greg made a seat with their locked arms and hoisted me up the stairs into the house. We sat once again on the beautiful porch watching the hummingbirds take off and land again on the many bird feeders. One little guy flew right into their picture window. He sat stunned on the back of the chair where he had landed. I knew exactly how the little guy felt.

I listened to Jean's account of how she was healed. After moving to the mountains it took her a year to acclimate to the high altitude and get her strength back. She then asked the Lord what He wanted her to do and God opened a door for her to teach a Bible study for women. That was such an encouragement to me that God might choose to use my trials to encourage others. I hugged them both and Mr. Bolton told me to "Hang on." Those two little words were exactly what I needed to hear. You really don't have to say much to someone that is hurting. I've learned that a hug or smile or just someone to sit and listen is often enough.

We left their house and went back to the campground. On the way back we called Dr. John in Houston to give him a report on how things were going. He thought I should have been better by this time (so did we). What he said next took us both by surprise. He directed Greg to take me somewhere lower in altitude like Las Cruces. He felt like I had probably experienced altitude sickness which would have been an extra burden on my body making me feel worse.

"Where in the world is Las Cruces?" we asked the park owners. They informed us that it was southwest of Cloudcroft, across White Sands desert and over another mountain range. Given the crazy turn of events, we turned again to prayer (as you can tell by now, we survived this trip through tons of prayer, and a heaping dose of God's grace).

Greg called ahead and made a reservation at a hotel in Las Cruces. After purchasing a map, we waved goodbye to the kind people in the RV park. They had treated us like family, and told Greg that they would clean up the trailer and get it back to the Bolton's. It was a bit overwhelming for us to pick up and move again. We were so discouraged that I cried as we drove by moonlight away from the charming town of Cloudcroft. We had hoped the clean and cool mountain air would be a benefit, but it seemed to have backfired. Yet, we had been ministered to in the most amazing and unusual ways. We were made to feel like family by total strangers. As we turned out onto the highway, it felt like I was leaving a little bit of my heart behind.

The Lord knew it was a desire of mine to see an elk before leaving the mountains. With tears still in my eyes I looked up to my left and saw him, standing majestically on the side of the road—one of God's most magnificent creatures! What a picture of strength this animal was with his enormous antlers. As we slowed down to get a good look, he stared at us as if to say, everything would be okay. Then he pranced gracefully into the valley. Somehow, seeing this beautiful elk gave me peace as we headed down the mountain into the desert night.

The drive was beautiful, especially as the full moon lit up expansive White Sands. It was sad however to leave the lush mountains and descend into the dry desert. As we drove, in the quiet of the night I thought, "You know God; nothing is ever ordinary with you." I've learned to buckle my seat belt and hold on tight because this journey with the Lord is a wild one. However, Jesus makes the journey worth it!

DAY 5

Remember your word to your servant, for you have given me hope. My comfort in my suffering is this: Your promise preserves my life. (Psalm 119:49-50)

I am lying in a hotel bed in a strange city in New Mexico, further from home than before, and among new strangers. At least in Cloudcroft, I had someone expecting me who I knew could identify with me. Here, there is no one. If I did not know my Lord, I would say He has turned His back on me. But I know whom I have believed in and I'm persuaded that He is able. (2 Timothy 1:12)

The pain has intensified today and I'm downright miserable. Doctor John wanted an update, so Greg called him mid-afternoon and reported that I had worsened. He advised Greg to take me to the emergency room for a chest x-ray and EKG. My weary husband got off the phone and wept. The last place he wanted to take me was another medical facility—we'd been down that road far too many times.

I know that Greg is absolutely worn out, and probably thinks that he has made one of the biggest mistakes of his life. Now it was impossible to imagine how I was going to fly back home.

What miracle would God send today? It was a phone call, where Greg learned that his best friend from San Antonio happened to be in El Paso on business. What are the odds? When his friend Pete heard about our dilemma, he insisted on driving to Las Cruces just to encourage and pray with us. What a blessing he was! It became so obvious that this was arranged by a loving God who knew how refreshing it would be to see a familiar face, in the midst of the unfamiliar. Greg was encouraged by his long-time friend, but as the day wore on, I continued to worsen.

DAY 6

"Lord, how am I going to get on a plane tomorrow? Please help me to trust you in this desert experience. I want to go home. I am so sick...last night was awful. I don't want to die out here! My heart feels like it is on fire. We need your wisdom. Do we go to the hospital? Do we even try to go home? Hang on to me Lord—I am crying out for deliverance. Father, sustain me according to your will; please fight for me. My children need their mommy! Heaven sounds wonderful, but what about Greg? How will he make it without me? I'm afraid. Help me not to fear. I believe you are not finished with me, and I want to live. Remember Matthew, Mary Kate, little Emma and my mom."

A few hours after I wrote this prayer, Greg anxiously drove me to the emergency room in Las Cruces. Seeing that I was profoundly weak the ER staff discerned the gravity of my situation, and got me back right away. I was in wretched shape, and it was only 10:00 a.m. The ER doctor had some blood tests run, all of which came back normal. He determined that the severe pain was probably from chest wall inflammation associated with lupus, and ordered a large dose of steroid to be pushed through intravenously.

After the I.V. was removed, they prepared to release me. Greg and the nurse were trying to put on my shoes when I suddenly began to grow faint. Within seconds, I could not even hold up my head, much less walk. The doctor had already discharged me but I could not seem to move on my own. Greg wanted me to move, the nurse and the doctor wanted me to, but I absolutely could not. My eyelids felt like they weighed five pounds each and I was unable to focus. My entire body began to shake as I tried to lift my head. I remember thinking, "Am I collapsing?" It was a dreadful feeling of impending doom. I just kept saying the name of Jesus, trying to calm my body and emotions. My children's faces flashed before my eyes as tears rolled down. "So this is what it feels like to die," I thought. Then a wave of the Lord's presence and grace flowed over me.

After the medical team struggled to get me up, they realized I was not getting better. In fact, my situation was declining. The emergency room was very busy that day, and because they needed the room, they wheeled my bed into what looked like a closet and closed the door. It was actually a very small room, with just enough space for the bed and one chair.

There was no nurse to check on my condition, nor was I monitored. It seemed heartless. I felt rejected and forgotten and at that moment, I was reminded of how Christ must have felt when He was rejected. Even though I was unable to speak, I told the Lord in my mind to fight for me. I wanted to be home in the Houston Medical Center for the first time in my life. Surely they would not push me off in a closet to suffer. I wanted to scream, "I'm not crazy!" What happened next was nothing short of miraculous, as God sent someone who would turn our despair into hope.

A petite lady slipped into the room and came to my bedside. She introduced herself as Naomi, and I actually thought she was an angel sent from God to comfort to me. I found that my new friends in Cloudcroft had called her because she lived in Las Cruces. This lovely woman held my hand and sang to me, "It Is Well with My Soul" and "I Need Thee Every Hour."

She was so loving and compassionate, exuding the love of Christ to both of us with her words and her songs. After praying for us, she noticed how cold I was and decided to drive back home to make me some soup. Naomi returned, smuggling the warm soup into the hospital where she fed me because I was too weak to even hold a spoon. This was the second time on our trip that I was fed soup by a stranger. But they really weren't strangers at all. Jean, Bob, Mary

Alice, the owners of the RV park, the couple who had helped us get oxygen and Naomi, were all servants of the Lord. They were family—our brothers and sisters in Christ—and we could feel it strongly.

We kissed and hugged Naomi when it was time to say goodbye. She was a miracle in our moment of anguish. God is so faithful to deliver His servants in times of trials. He is able to take care of his children and provide for them anywhere, at any time and in every situation. He is Jehovah Jireh, the Lord our provider.

Finally, after hours of waiting, a new doctor came in to see me. By this time, I felt a little stronger and could talk again. Thankfully this doctor took my concerns seriously. He listened very carefully, and could tell that I was weak. The plan was for me to be kept overnight for observation, so a nurse came and moved me across the hall and started to monitor me again. It took four attempts to get a new I.V. started. But at least the nurse was kind, with a deep compassion in his eyes which gave me additional comfort.

In addition to the painful inflammation, the diagnosis was that my electrolytes were way out of balance, my blood pressure was terribly low and I was dehydrated. The pain medication caused an allergic reaction where my lips began to swell, and eventually my throat started to close. I now had difficulty swallowing and breathing, so the nurse promptly administered an antihistamine intravenously.

DAY 7

Greg was beyond exhausted by this time - (I am now convinced that I'm responsible for every grey hair on his head). It was the hardest thing for him to leave me in a strange hospital at midnight in the middle of the desert. I understood that he needed to go back to the hotel for some much-needed sleep. He had been right by my side through everything, only stepping out to call friends and family, and to reschedule our return flight. I was afraid for him to leave, but I drew comfort in knowing that the Great Physician would take care of me. I remember looking over at the empty chair beside my bed, knowing without a doubt that it was occupied by Jesus himself, or one worn out angel. I clutched the cross around my neck reading the small print on the back, "It was then that I carried you." I knew the Lord was carrying me now.

After Greg left, I overheard a man cursing at his wife over the phone, telling her to come get him. He became louder and louder, so filled with rage and anger that it frightened me. I had to remind myself several times that I was protected by Almighty God, and I truly found refuge under His wings until the danger had passed. Quietly, I began to pray for the man. He started to pace the halls, walking past the room where I was lying, feeling vulnerable and paralyzed. The male nurse told him that he must go back to his room. When he refused, Michael, (my nurse) called out loudly for security. The man shouted angrily that he did not have to go back to his room. He was out of control, and of course his room was right beside mine! Because of all the commotion, I'm quite sure I no longer had low blood pressure.

"God help me, will this saga ever end?" I prayed quietly. Before long, several security personnel tackled the large man and pushed him up against the wall. There was a struggle, and I just knew at any second they were going to burst through the wall and land in my bed! My prayers were no longer quiet as I prayed for strength for the nurses and security, and protection for us all. The irate man cursed, yelling continually at Michael, "I will sue you!" His wife, who had arrived in the meantime, told him, "You will not – just shut up!"

Thank God, they finally moved me upstairs to a private room. To say that I was relieved to get out of that emergency room would be a huge understatement. It had been a long and unbelievable twelve hours. Who in the world would ever believe me if I told them what my day had been like? It felt like I had been to hell and back, with an angel visit in the middle!

Upstairs was like an oasis compared to the emergency room below. I finally began to get drowsy from the effects of the pain medicine, coupled with sheer exhaustion. I was in a real room and I felt safe. Before falling asleep I prayed:

"Thank you, Lord, for medicines when we need them. Thank you for rescuing me unharmed from the battle waged against me. Thank you Jesus for saving my life today! I believe I was in danger. Thank you for hundreds of people who prayed across several different states. I ask that you bless each one who got on their knees for me."There is mighty power in prayer.

DAY 8

Because of the LORD's great love we are not consumed, for his compassions never fail. They are new every morning; great is your faithfulness.
(Lamentations 3:22-23)

It is a new day. I am ALIVE, and feeling stronger by the hour. Praise the Lord! The doctor is ready to release me, though I'm a little nervous because of flashbacks from yesterday. The whole ordeal seems surreal. Getting home to my children is my number one goal. I miss them terribly. I am apprehensive about driving back to El Paso and flying home, but I must believe that God will make a way. Look what He just brought us through. If I cannot trust Him after this experience, I have learned nothing.

How quickly we can forget the miracles God does for us. We ask Him to part the Red Sea for us and He does; but sometimes not the way we expect Him too. I had made this trip asking and hoping for healing, but the Lord chose to apply His healing touch on the inside.

I have been waiting for a miracle in my body when God has been trying to show me all along that He was performing one in my heart. "Forgive me Lord, for I am slow to see these things. Thank you for the miracles you have done in my life and in my heart."

Before I was discharged, a hospital Chaplain stopped by for a visit. She selected I Peter 5:6 –7 to share with me. "*Humble yourselves therefore, under God's mighty hand, that he may lift you up in due time. Cast all your anxiety on him because he cares for you.*"

Shortly after, they wheeled me out to the car, where Greg was waiting to drive me back to the hotel. The next morning, we made the trip down to El Paso, and caught our flight home. My children and weary in-laws met us at the Houston airport. During the seizure-like episode in the hospital, I honestly believed that I would never see my children again this side of heaven. Upon seeing their precious faces, I hugged them with all the strength I had left.

I felt like Dorothy from "The Wizard of Oz," repeating: "There's no place like home! There's no place like home! There's no place like home."

Lessons learned from our trip:

1. God is faithful to provide for his children anywhere and everywhere.

2. The Lord desires for us to completely surrender our lives to Him.

3. This surrender involves laying down our agendas, our plans, and our ideas to His Sovereign will.

4. Our Father in heaven loves us His children, more than we will ever know.

5. We can trust Jesus when we are completely alone in the desert.

6. We can rest in Him, even when afraid.

7. God sustains us in the dark.

8. I realized how deeply I love my husband who went through this, and so much more by my side.

What I Learned Lying Down

Chapter 13

Life on the Farm

Blessed is the man who perseveres under trial, because when he has stood the test, he will receive the crown of life that God has promised to those who love him. (James 1:12)

Following our disastrous, yet miraculous trip to New Mexico, I became disheartened. God had grown our faith, along with teaching us many other lessons; and the trip had yielded fruit, just not the kind we had anticipated. The decision was made; our roots would remain in Texas, at least for the time being.

Once again I encountered heart palpitations, intense pain and weakness along with a monstrous flare-up. My overall condition took a sharp nose dive, with most of my time spent in bed on strong pain medications and oxygen. One particular night, I felt as though death was closing in, so I asked God, "What is going to happen to me?" I heard two words, *"Trust Me."*

In the days that followed, I experienced a growing sense that somehow I had brought this illness and misery on my family, and my mood began to reflect that I was succumbing to this lie from the enemy. One evening, Greg handed me an envelope from our mailbox with no return address. On a small piece of paper inside was this typewritten message: John 11:4.

"This sickness will not end in death. No, it is for God's glory that God's Son may be glorified through it." I remember thinking…"God sends mail?"

Oh, how I needed that timely word from the Lord at that moment. This verse provided unbelievable comfort for years to come and I treasured it, and hid it in my heart. God knew I would need this encouragement for the journey ahead. Just two weeks later, we received an invitation that would change our lives.

Doctor John, who had asked us to consider going to New Mexico, now had an offer to make to us. He invited me to come live on his farm about 70 miles northwest of Houston. He felt that a less drastic move, one that would get me away from the city pollution and into the country air, might help.

Leaving the comforts of home and everything that I knew and loved, we accepted Doctor John's offer and followed his advice. I packed up and moved to his guest house bringing little Emma along. Since Greg still had his full-time job in Houston, and our other two children were enrolled in elementary school there, they could only visit on weekends. It saddened me to part with them each Sunday, knowing that I wouldn't see them for another week. Emma and I would have to brave the country and the critters together. (Did I mention that the only pet my kids ever had up to this point was a duck?)

Dr. John's farm was populated with longhorn cattle, beautiful horses, dogs, cats, goldfish and a donkey named "Don Key Haute" (think Man of La Mancha). Of course a farm would not be complete without coyotes, armadillos, rats, roadrunners, scorpions, snakes and Texas-sized bugs!

You know that you are living on a farm when your alarm clock is a donkey heehawing outside your window, and the first thing you grab in the morning is *not* your coffee, but a fly swatter. Moving from suburbia to a working farm was an adventure that would change our family forever. During our time there, we learned many valuable lessons, although some were bittersweet. God had thrown us an unexpected curve ball that set our lives in a whole new direction.

My doctor and his wife were so generous to offer their two-room guesthouse free of charge, as long as needed. This was ample room for me and Emma, who was four years old, but when all five of us were there it became very close quarters.

We went from a five bedroom, four bath house to a two room house; one big bedroom up, one big family room down (kitchen, dining and living all in one). There were zero bathtubs, one toilet and a shower. We went from a laundry room with washer and dryer in the house, to a washer and dryer in the barn; automatic dishwasher to hand-washing; a busy street to a gravel road; one quarter acre to fifty acres; city noise to serenity; smoggy skies to stars galore; flat plains to rolling hills and bare feet to boots.

The small two-story frame house was built on the side of a hill where you could not miss the beauty of the rising and setting sun. At night, you could see a great distance, and I loved to gaze out the upstairs window, thinking of our Grand Creator. It was during this time that Matthew 5:14 came alive in my heart. *"You are the light of the world. A city on a hill cannot be hidden."* This prompted me to pray that our family would be like city on a hill, shining in the darkness for all to see—not for our glory but for the glory of the Lord.

After a few weeks of country living I began to improve, although still far from well. Palpitations left after the first few nights and I was stronger, no longer needing the oxygen! For one week, I thought God had used the farm to heal me. Dr. John believed that the power lines, pollution of the city, and other environmental irritants had been greatly affecting my immune system.

Separated from my home, my bed and bathtub, my things, friends, church family and even my children and husband at times, it felt like God had turned me upside down; shaking the material world and it's trappings from the core of me. This was one of those really tough lessons in dying to self (I called this one a radical crash course). It was as if the Lord whispered, *"Leave everything behind and wholly depend on Me – more of Jesus, less of Angie."* I was the Lord's instrument and He was my teacher. I followed Him and He led me. Although dark and difficult, the Lord was faithful to supply His grace and comfort when I became sick again.

March 17, 2006

Today I'm utterly miserable –Weakness, fatigue, chest pain, congestion and discouragement threaten to take me under. I was in bed all day long. My family was in and out trying to let me rest. I'm alone and isolated in a place foreign to me; cut off from the outside world. I miss the sun, my friends, my home of ten years and my church. If left in this state, I believe I would go insane. From morning till evening I'm shut in the four walls of this small house, and just when I think I might lose it, God shows me his love in a really sweet way. Greg decided to serve communion for our family. It was a comfort, but I barely had the strength to sit at the table. Finally, feeling at the end of my rope, I laid my head down on my arms and quietly began to cry. I try so hard not to let my children see my tears, however, I have learned that it is okay for our children to see us cry. Mary was sitting beside me and gently took my head in her small hands stroking my hair. Matthew then helped me to the couch and covered me with a blanket. He then sat down to write on his magnetic drawing board: God loves us all – God cares for us – He will never leave us. Then Emma came to me, cocked her head to one side and said, "I want to comfort you Mommy." She decided the best way to do this was to load me down with her favorite stuffed animals and her blanket. How ironic, this reminded me when Mary was four and brought her stuffed bear and blanket to my bed for me to sleep with. Oh, Lord I just want my kids to know what it is like to have a healthy mother…even if only for a short time. That night, it surely felt like I was hanging by a thread. I held my Bible close to my heart as I slept – The Lord had delivered me through one more day.

While my health was still rocky, we had experienced some periods of relief on the farm. Thus after about two months, and much prayer, my husband finally decided that living out of the city was better for me than living in it. Around Christmas, Greg and the older kids moved themselves and the bare essentials to the farm house.

For four months our family of five lived in this little house with one bathroom, one bedroom and one closet. Our clothes were stacked on the floor next to the kids' makeshift beds, and when I tucked Emma in at night the Lord would whisper, *"This is only temporary."* All five of us slept in one large room, or should I say, attempted to. Being a light sleeper I got the least rest. Mary talked and walked in her sleep, Emma often let out dramatic sighs, Greg snored, but thank goodness Matthew slept quietly.

Strangely, this sleeping arrangement would be something that I would later miss when we finally moved our family into a new house. In fact, when we settled into our new home it felt odd to me for us to sleep in separate bedrooms! The Lord spoke to me loud and clear that life on earth is not about our comfort.

The Lord did not call us to a life of ease; seasons of testing and trials are painful. The wilderness experience can be long and uncomfortable, but take heart, it is passable! The good news is that when we are placed in the fire, Jesus goes with us. We were certainly out of our comfort zone, but God was so good to balance out the stress with unexpected joys.

The animals on the farm provided stress relief and entertainment. From the kitchen window I watched the cattle and their calves, and through another window, the beautiful horses. Our time on the farm taught us the beauty and freedom of a simple life.

When we needed smiles and laughter, we watched Nellie, the sheep dog, chase Donkey around the little house and then vice versa. This adorable donkey was a mess, playfully harassing us. Once, while walking to the barn with a load of laundry, he quietly followed me. Then he grabbed the back of my jacket with his teeth, and to my surprise and alarm, my bra came unhooked! I learned to watch my back after that incident and Greg learned to keep an eye out for the unexpected too.

One night after some friends from our home church came to visit and pray, Greg walked to the end of the long gravel driveway to close the gate for the night. He said he started walking faster and faster because he heard something scampering behind him. As dark as it was, he could not tell which nocturnal animal it was. Eventually he broke into a full-fledged sprint to the house. Unknown to us until that night, an armadillo lived under the house that we occupied—so they were both running home! I'll never forget how pale Greg looked as he slammed the door behind him. Farm life was surely an adjustment for the five of us.

Our conversation changed drastically as well. Instead of: "Kids, watch for cars", it became, "Kids, watch out for cow patties." "Girls, stop tasting the horse feed!" "Where are your boots?" "Where is the fly swatter?" "No, that is not a kitty, it's a skunk!" It seems comical now, but at the time this former "city girl" felt like she could come unglued at any moment.

Because of the initial improvement of my health and a tug from the Lord, we put our home on the market. After this decision, and after we had transferred the kids to a school not far from the farm, the disease ramped up considerably. The Lord told me at this time, *"This is not about you."* This helped me to know, but we were still hard pressed on every side. It appeared that we were surrounded by confusion and we needed the Lord to make our crooked places straight (Isaiah 45:2).

This decision to move permanently took a gigantic leap of faith, given that we were leaving behind a wonderful support system, which included our church, friends and neighbors that we loved dearly, along with our home. By human standards, this seemed illogical and many questioned our rationale hoping to talk us out of the move, but we knew this was something that God was directing. We were walking by faith, not by sight.

Multi-tasking became a way of life for my husband. With the kids changing schools mid-year, and Greg's commute now over an hour, he was stretched like silly putty in every conceivable direction. Nevertheless, we were humbled because of God's faithfulness to provide all that we needed.

Can you believe a second grade teacher lived next door to the farm? In our neck of the woods, next door was a quarter mile away. Since Greg had such a long commute, she began taking my kids to their new school and brought them home each day.

This sweet lady was a specific answer to prayer. Ironically, she would also be Mary's second grade teacher. God once again demonstrated how He paved the road before us, supplying our every need. The Lord knew we needed help with transportation, so he placed a friend next door to drive them for me. What an amazing God!

My doctor and his sweet wife occupied their farmhouse on weekends, which was just up the hill from the guest house. It was odd to see him on the farm. For years, I had only known him in a white lab coat and stethoscope, but now he was a cowboy on a tractor. Not odd for him of course, but an escape from working with difficult patients like me to tending to cows and horses who did not tell you their problems. As time went by, I got quite used to seeing him in jeans feeding the cattle or driving his John Deere.

Our appointments were no longer in the urban office, but outside the little guest house where I sat in the evening. He would walk by with a sack of feed thrown over his shoulder, or leading one of the horses to the barn, stopping by to ask how I was doing. How often do you hear of a doctor taking in their sick patients? He and his wife became our friends, along with his mother who was the ranch manager when they were away during the week. We loved walking up the hill to the main house to sit in the rocking chairs on the front porch, and visit with this family over an occasional bowl of ice cream. We are so grateful for this family who took us in when we were in need.

Eventually, we were able to move away from the farm. Although we miss old friends, we have grown to love our new place and the town that the Lord led us to. God has been faithful to provide a new support system, along with many other blessings. Greg was able to keep his job, and thankfully he commutes some days and telecommutes on others.

We've joined an amazing group of believers who surround us with love and are all about ministering to our community and leading people to Christ. Praise God, our children are excelling and they are witnesses to the faithfulness of God wherever they go.

Living on the farm certainly bonded our family like nothing else ever had. We were far from the city distractions and noise, so we found other interests like: star gazing and Friday night dominoes. These activities gave us a taste of the simpler life that we still enjoy today.

Unexpected blessings were found on the farm; however we were still engaged in daily spiritual warfare. So over time, the Lord taught me how to be strong in Him. In the next chapter, we will shift gears and I will share with you about *how* He has equipped us to withstand the battle.

What I Learned Lying Down

Chapter 14

Fighting with My Sword

For though we live in the world, we do not wage war as the world does. The weapons we fight with are not the weapons of the world. On the contrary, they have divine power to demolish strongholds. (2 Corinthians 10:3-4)

On the front line of battle you must be prepared. The soldier carefully puts on his uniform: headgear, vest, belt, combat boots and the necessary weapons. I am a soldier. Not your typical soldier, but a soldier none the less. I wear a belt, a breast plate, and special shoes; in addition, I am armed with a mighty shield, helmet and a double-edged sword. God has taught me to stand by putting on this armor daily and how to fight this battle by pure necessity. This is not a physical battle but a spiritual one; the weapons that I fight with are not the weapons of the world, but mighty against a very real enemy...Satan.

Our adversary the devil is the father of lies who wants to steal, kill and destroy. The Bible describes him prowling around as a roaring lion seeking whom he may devour. He delights in keeping us bound in sin, fear, doubts and insecurities. His desire is for the children of God to live in defeat so we can't be used to our full potential for the Lord and His kingdom. Remember, God wants us to be victors, not victims. Satan bombarded me with his "fiery darts" when I was completely caught off guard. Having experienced much time as his victim, my hope for you is that this chapter will help you to be strong in the Lord, equipped for the battle that we all face. I am praying for you, and the Lord is with you mighty warrior (Judges 6:12)!

Finally, be strong in the Lord and in his mighty power. Put on the full armor of God so that you can take your stand against the devil's schemes. For our struggle is not against flesh and blood, but against the rulers, against the authorities, against the powers of this dark world and against the spiritual forces of evil in the heavenly realms. (Ephesians 6:10-12)

Precious friends, most of us spend way too much time dressing the outer man, but little or no time dressing the spiritual inner man. You wouldn't think of walking outside without a coat in a snow storm. We must be more prepared on the inside, dressed for the battle waged against us every day.

Spiritual warfare is as real as the words on this page, and my family and I have experienced it firsthand. Hammered with depression and thoughts of despair, I was tempted to overdose on pills to end it all. Numerous times, wanting to die, I begged God to take me home.

I remember one evening feeling broken and oppressed, sobbing and looking out the window at the dirt in the flower bed. It looked so inviting, and the thought that I could not shake was a longing to be buried under it. It seemed like God was allowing Satan to destroy me, my marriage and my family. Falling to my face I would plead with God to fight for me. When we are vulnerable, weak or sick, Satan sees this as prime time to pelt us with guilt and lies only to bring more misery and pain. My battle was spiritual, emotional and physical, and the assault was felt on all sides.

Because a big part of the battle was going on in my mind, I was often deceived. I doubted myself repeatedly and condemnation and guilt were my constant companions. The disease I was fighting was intense and my exhausted husband plus three needy children were also struggling with health issues, depression and anxiety. The good news was and is that the Lord never left us and He won't leave you either!

Even writing this book has been an ordeal because of the outside forces that are against this message. In order to survive this war launched against me there was no option, I *had* to learn to stand.

Trying to make it through each day I used "the sword", speaking God's Word out loud at every turn. But why did I still feel beat up and battle weary? Wasn't God fighting for me? Something was missing; I *knew* there had to be more. It was then that the Lord showed me in order to stand I needed to pick up the other five pieces of protection; they all work together. He never intended for us to fight in our own strength; that is a recipe for disaster. The Lord is our strength. He does fight for us. We stand firm. I praise God for what he taught me while sitting at His feet, discovering the treasures of His beautiful armor.

Therefore put on the full armor of God, so that when the day of evil comes, you may be able to stand your ground, and after you have done everything, to stand. Stand firm then with the belt of truth buckled around your waist, with the breastplate of righteousness in place, and with your feet fitted with the readiness that comes from the gospel of peace. In addition to all this, take up the shield of faith, with which you can extinguish all the flaming arrows of the evil one. Take the helmet of salvation and the sword of the Spirit, which is the Word of God. And pray in the Spirit on all occasions with all kinds of prayers and requests. With this in mind, be alert and always keep on praying for all the saints. (Ephesians 6:13-18)

Out of dire need God called me to study the armor, and naturally I thought the focus would be on our enemy. Instead I found that it magnifies our precious Lord Jesus! He is the truth, our righteousness, our peace, our shield, our salvation, and the living Word.

As I read these verses the word "stand" jumped out at me. God always has significance in repetition. Being a mom of three, I repeat myself constantly, in hopes that my children will remember what I have instructed them to do. It is no different with God; He is our Father and we are His children.

Sitting on the floor in pajamas one night, with Bible, concordance and notes strewn everywhere, excitement welled up in me. It was one of those light bulb moments. If my family hadn't been asleep I probably would have shouted with joy as the Holy Spirit reminded me of this verse. It felt like puzzle pieces were coming together and God was giving me answers to my questions:

...Do not be afraid or discouraged because of this vast army. For the battle is not yours, but God's...You will not have to fight this battle. Take up your positions; stand firm and see the deliverance the LORD will give you. (2 Chronicles 20: 15 & 17)

Remember that we just read the verse about putting on the full armor so that when the day of evil comes we may be able to stand. Friends, we are able to stand firm by putting on, piece by piece, this full suit of armor.

He put on righteousness as his breastplate, and the helmet of salvation on his head; he put on the garments of vengeance and wrapped himself in zeal as in a cloak. (Isaiah 59:17)

Praise the LORD, O my soul. O LORD my God, you are very great; you are clothed with splendor and majesty. He wraps himself in light as with a garment, he stretches out the heavens like a tent. (Psalm104: 1-2)

So let us put aside the deeds of darkness and put on the armor of light. (Romans 13:12)

Jesus is the light and in Him there is no darkness. *Our spiritual armor is Christ.* This was absolutely profound to me as I meditated on this thought. We are strong in the Lord when we put on Christ and His power! Each morning I pray, reminding myself of all six pieces and their function. This is also a precious time of thanking God for His truth, His righteousness, His peace, His gift of faith, salvation and His Word.

Come along with me as we uncover treasures and learn more about this mysterious armor. Are you ready to get dressed? These are life-changing garments that will never wear out. Of course we are not literally putting on this gear, but figuratively placing on the attributes of Christ. Let's begin with a look at the first piece that we are to fasten on.

The Belt of Truth

Stand firm then, with the belt of truth buckled around your waist... (Ephesians 6:14)

Roman soldiers wore a knee length garment called a tunic that was belted at the waist. The belt was very important for several reasons, one being that the sword, and sometimes the breastplate were attached to it. The King James Bible speaks of girding up your loins. That meant that a soldier had to tuck his tunic into his belt to keep from tripping. Without the truth we will trip and fall. Without the truth we cannot be saved. But with the truth, the veil is lifted and we are given abundant life.

Truth is our foundation and most powerful weapon. With deception around every corner, we should have this truth wrapped around us every day. Otherwise, we will be taken in by something disguised as the truth, such as false teaching. The truth sets us free and guards us from deception.

These verses also mention the schemes of the devil or the wiles of the devil. Remember the Saturday morning cartoon featuring Wile E. Coyote and the Roadrunner? The coyote did everything he could to set a trap and trick the roadrunner. With the truth and this vital armor we can survive the traps set for us because *"No weapon that is formed against you will prosper"* (Isaiah 54:17 NASB).

It has been helpful for me, when putting the armor on each morning, to speak out loud a few verses relating to each piece. I believe it reinforces my position in Christ and I feel stronger and taller after placing on the full suit.

We will still have difficulties and battles in this life, especially as followers of Christ. The great Apostle Paul wrote the book of Ephesians while in prison. It has been said that he was probably looking at the Roman soldier guarding him while he wrote these God-inspired verses.

Despite trials and tribulations we can have peace, joy and victory. We are covered when we put on Christ, for there is no better protection. We are truly hidden in Him. Hallelujah! Here is something to think about: I did a study on the word "truth" and counted approximately eighty times in the gospels where Jesus said, "I tell you the truth." Jesus *cannot* lie—He is Truth itself.

The Bible also has this to say about the truth:

The truth will set you free. (John 8:32)

Jesus is the way, the truth, and the life. (John 14:6)

The Holy Spirit is the Spirit of truth. (John 14:17)

The Word is truth. (John 17:17)

Jesus is called Faithful and True. (Rev. 19:11)

I, the LORD, speak the truth; I declare what is right (Isaiah 45:19).

Satan is the father of lies and the author of confusion so sometimes his lies sound like truth; however, God's truth can defeat Satan's lies. When the truth sets you free the Lord makes all things new. That includes a garment of salvation and a beautiful robe of righteousness!

The Breastplate of Righteousness

...with the breastplate of righteousness in place...
(Ephesians 6:14)

The breastplate protected a soldier's vital organs, such as the heart and lungs. He was able to boldly approach the enemy because his heart was covered. I think of this righteousness as our bullet-proof vest. Because of His righteousness, we can come boldly with confidence to the throne of grace. To be honest, I feel inadequate in attempting to explain this righteousness because it feels like holy ground to me. I pray that these verses will convey what I cannot.

God made him who had no sin to be sin for us, so that in him we might become the righteousness of God. (2 Corinthians 5:21)

This righteousness is undeserved and unearned, given to us based on our salvation. When we repent of our sin and accept Jesus as our Savior, we receive the incredible gift of His righteousness! Meditating on this completely overwhelms me. How do you describe something that you can hardly wrap your mind around? This has been called "The Great Exchange." Our filthy sin-stained garments, in exchange for His white linen robe of righteousness – I know this seems unbelievable, but it is true.

I delight greatly in the LORD; my soul rejoices in my God. For He has clothed me with garments of salvation and arrayed me in a robe of righteousness,

*as a bridegroom adorns his head like a priest, and as
a bride adorns herself with her jewels.* (Isaiah 61:10)

In my life, His righteousness has been so powerful in
protecting me from the condemnation that Satan loves to heap
on us. If you personally know Jesus –then you are the
righteousness of God! Regardless of what your past may be,
there is now no condemnation for those who are in Christ
Jesus. For the law of the Spirit of life in Christ Jesus has set
you free from the law of sin and death (Romans 8:1-2 NASB).

Putting on this righteousness by faith, I pray asking God
to guard my heart and emotions. Of course, it should also
remind us to live upright and holy lives.

*You were taught, with regard to your former way of
life to put off your old self which is being corrupted
by its deceitful desires; to be made new in the attitude
of your minds; and to put on the new self, created to
be like God in true righteousness and holiness.*
(Ephesians 4:22-24)

We are to follow the example of Christ and live a life
pleasing to the Lord by living out His righteousness. This
righteousness is a picture us of His unfailing love for us. *"This
is love: not that we loved God, but that he loved us and sent
his Son as an atoning sacrifice for our sins"* (1 John 4:10).
What a Savior!

Knowing our position in Christ is imperative when
standing against our enemy. We have to know who we are
before we can stand. Satan is skilled in reminding us of our
failures and mistakes, so we have to renew our minds with the
truth of our identity in Christ.

In Christ, we are:

Blessed with every spiritual blessing (Ephesians 1:3)

Holy and blameless (Ephesians 1:4)

Predestined to be adopted (Ephesians 1:5)

Redeemed and forgiven (Ephesians 1:7)

Sealed by the Holy Spirit (Ephesians 1:13)

Made alive (Ephesians 2:5)

Seated in the heavenly realms (Ephesians 2:6)

God's workmanship (Ephesians 2:10)

Given access to the Father (Ephesians 2:18)

Citizens of heaven and members of God's household (Ephesians 2:19)

Able to approach God with freedom and confidence (Ephesians 3:12)

In each of my children's bedrooms there is a list of similar verses so they will be continually reminded of their position in Christ. It has been one of the most powerful ways to encourage both my children and myself.

As I studied each piece of armor, I was amazed at the order of the pieces and how each one leads to another, for example: *"The fruit of righteousness will be peace; the effect of righteousness will be quietness and confidence forever"* (Isaiah 32:17).

The Shoes of Peace

... and with your feet fitted (or shod) with the readiness that comes from the gospel of peace.
(Ephesians 6:15)

Roman soldiers wore thick-soled boots with metal cleats. These shoes allowed them to march over difficult terrain. This brings to my mind our walk with the Lord. Paul describes this journey as a race to be run (1 Corinthians 9:24). He also challenges us to forget what is behind and reach forward to what lies ahead with our goal being Christ, and the prize eternal life (Philippians 3:13).

Our journey on earth is often long and difficult, marked with joy and pain. It sometimes takes us to rugged, steep and dangerous places, through deep valleys, dry deserts and high mountains. But there is One who walks beside us. Mighty storms will threaten to take us under, however we can stand firm in these storms, when we fix our eyes on Jesus, the Prince of Peace.

Jesus was my peace through the physical abuse of my first husband, and through the divorce that followed. He was my peace when my father died of cancer just three weeks before my baby girl was born. His peace surrounded me when I had an emergency delivery and my life was in danger.

When diagnosed with lupus, a life threatening disease, His peace covered me. When doctors tested me for a rare cancer, it was His peace that held me. Through ambulance rides, chronic pain, a broken marriage and sick children, Jesus was my peace.

Just before Jesus was crucified He told the disciples He would send another Counselor to be with them; the Spirit of truth (John 14:16-17). The Holy Spirit is the Spirit of truth. Jesus goes on to speak this beautiful verse of comfort: *"Peace I leave with you; my peace I give you. I do not give to you as the world gives. Do not let your hearts be troubled and do not be afraid"* (vs.27).

In a world full of chaos and fear how does the believer remain peaceful and unafraid? Daily Bible reading is critical to our peace, and of course, prayer and meditation yield peace. Think on verses such as:

> *"Do not be anxious about anything, but in everything, by prayer and petition, with thanksgiving present your requests to God. And the peace of God which transcends all understanding, will guard your hearts and your minds in Christ Jesus"* (Phil. 4:6-7).

Peace is also a fruit of the Spirit (Galatians 5:22). In the gospel of John, Chapter 15 there is a parable where Jesus compares himself to a vine, and the followers of Christ to fruitful branches. We produce this fruit by abiding in Christ and walking in obedience. Read these strong words of Jesus below:

> *Abide in Me, and I in you. As the branch cannot bear fruit of itself unless it abides in the vine, so neither can you unless you abide in Me. I am the vine, you are the branches; he who abides in Me and I in him,*

he bears much fruit, for apart from Me you can do nothing. (John 15:4, 5 NASB)

A branch cannot grow separated from the vine, it will wither and die. So it is with us, we must not depart from Jesus as He is our source of life, strength, peace and joy. Jesus said that if we obey His commands we will remain in His love and His joy will be in us and our joy will be complete (John 15:10-11). Obedience is the key to abiding.

In our journey, our feet will not always march forward, sometimes the Lord will have us stand still and wait on Him. It is during this time that He teaches us to *"Be still and know that I am God..."* (Psalm 46:10).

Experienced at being still, I know exactly how difficult this is. I eventually learned that in stillness we can find treasures, hear His gentle whisper and learn His truths. If your life is at a standstill, and it seems you have no purpose, be encouraged. God acts on behalf of those who wait (Isaiah 64:4). Many times we can't see how God is using our difficulty to affect the life of someone watching.

God has called us to share the good news wherever we go. My girls and I love to tell people that Jesus loves them. The smiles we receive from speaking these three wonderful words are heartwarming. Last week, I got a kiss on the cheek from an elderly woman that needed to hear it! That was a first. Look for opportunities to show Jesus to the lost world around you. Each of us should, *"Always be prepared to give an answer to everyone who asks you to give the reason for the hope that you have. But do this with gentleness and respect..."* (1 Peter 3:15).

You were born for such a time as this and He has given you a mission. God chose you, He loves you. His desire is for you and I to tell others of this free gift. Jesus is coming soon so our time is short. We can be fruitful in our suffering by sharing the gospel – the good news that Jesus died for you and me and rose from the dead.

As warriors, let us put on the whole armor of God by faith. When we put on these shoes they are a reminder of the peace that we must walk in and take with us wherever we go.

> *How beautiful on the mountains are the feet of those who bring good news, who proclaim peace, who bring good tidings, who proclaim salvation...* (Isaiah 52:7)

We are halfway there; now we must take up the next three pieces.

The Shield of Faith

> *In addition to all this, take up the shield of faith, with which you can extinguish all the flaming arrows of the evil one.* (Ephesians 6:16)

The shield was the first line of defense for the Roman soldier, and it is ours as well. Soldiers carried rectangular shields that were four feet high by two feet wide. Before battle, the leather that covered the shield was wet down in order to put out the flaming arrows. When soldiers stood side by side they would link their shields together, forming a shelter or line of defense, as it has been called. This served to protect so they could move forward to the front line in unity.

Following are beautiful verses to remind us *who* our shield is:

But you are a shield around me, O LORD; you bestow glory on me and lift up my head. (Psalm3:3)

The LORD is my strength and my shield; my heart trusts in him, and I am helped. (Psalm 28:7)

His faithfulness will be your shield and rampart. (Psalm 91:4)

You are my refuge and my shield; I have put my hope in your Word. (Psalm 119:114)

Faith is complete trust and belief in God. If we are to have faith we must believe His words.

Consequently, faith comes from hearing the message, and the message is heard through the word of Christ (Romans 10:17).

We are saved by grace through faith (Ephesians 2:8)

Faith is a gift from God (Ephesians 2:8)

We are to have child-like faith (Mark 10:15)

Our faith is strengthened by waiting (Romans 4:18-21)

We live by faith and not by sight (2 Corinthians 5:7)

Without faith it is impossible to please the Lord (Hebrews 11:6)

Our faith does not keep us from suffering or persecution (Hebrews 11:35-39)

Warren Wiersbe writes, His quiver is full of flaming arrows of adversity and he constantly bombards our defenses with the fiery darts. Frequently he fires a round of problems at us (sickness, financial loss, broken relationships) and then when our defenses are down, he hits us with his emotional darts of anger, fear, doubt, depression and self-pity. Without a strong line of defense, these arrows will hit their mark, and we will fall on the battlefield.[4]

These are wise and true words which I strongly identify with. Satan fires arrows of accusation, doubt, fear, guilt, discouragement, rejection, and condemnation. And they usually come at us quickly and without warning.

When I did not understand the chaos around me I would often say, "Lord, I will trust in you." I did not know at the time, but I was grabbing my shield and holding it up. Sure, there were times that doubt and fear prevailed, and I have felt the sting of many fiery darts, but I've learned that God can be trusted. He knows what is best for us. We can take Him at His word. By the Word of the Lord the heavens were made. "*For the word of the LORD is right and true; he is faithful in all he does*" (Psalm 33:4). May we all rest in His promises especially during these evil and difficult days that lie ahead.

We have nothing to fear as long as we take up the shield of faith – but when we begin to trust in our own strength, our shield comes down. Without him we can do nothing (John 15:5); *but we can do all things through Christ who gives us strength* (Philippians 4:13).

I have a very dear friend who calls me once a week to pray. It is one of the high points of my week. We laugh and cry while joining our hearts together in prayer for our families, our churches and our country. This is a special time of standing in agreement with one another and we have seen many answers to prayer. In Matthew 18:20, Jesus declared that where two or three come together in His name, He would be with them (even over the phone line).

Solomon wrote in Ecclesiastes chapter 4. *"Two are better than one, because they have a good return for their work: If one falls down his friend can help him up."* (vs. 9, 10) It goes on to say, *"Though one may be overpowered, two can defend themselves. A cord of three strands is not quickly broken."* (vs. 12) Great things happen when we are united in our faith. We are strengthened when we stand with other believers. *"As iron sharpens iron, so one man sharpens another"* (Proverbs 27:17). Connect with another believer and lift your shields high!

Jesus is our help and our shield, He rescues and He saves!

The Helmet of Salvation

Take the helmet of salvation and the sword of the Spirit, which is the word of God. (Ephesians 6:17)

The helmet was worn by the soldier to protect the head. The helmet of salvation protects our mind, which has been called "Satan's battleground."

Do not conform any longer to the pattern of this world, but be transformed by the renewing of your mind. Then you will be able to test and approve what

God's will is – his good, pleasing and perfect will.
(Romans 12:2)

The Bible tells us to prepare our minds for action, to be self-controlled and alert (1 Peter 1:13). I struggle to keep my mind focused, especially when I try to sit down to pray. Satan loves to distract us and will do anything to keep us from prayer. So we have to learn to take captive every thought and make it obedient to Christ (2 Corinthians 10:5). When taking up the helmet, it automatically reminds me to pray for my thoughts. I want my thoughts to glorify the Lord, which can be a real challenge at times. Praying the armor on each morning helps me to start off my day in a positive way, with each piece prompting me to pray for a specific area of my life.

I don't know about you, but my thoughts roam and my mind races. Since I can't go to and fro, my mind makes up for it, covering lots of miles. Today, my son is in Louisiana at church camp, my daughter is in Waco at another camp and my youngest is with her grandparents in San Antonio. When my mind needs a rest from worrying about them, I remind myself that The Lord has His eye on them. It takes real discipline to control this part of the flesh. In this battle for the mind, I often recite Philippians 4:8:

Finally brothers, whatever is true, whatever is noble, whatever is right, whatever is pure, whatever is lovely, whatever is admirable- if anything is excellent or praiseworthy think about such things.

Our goal should be to strive toward a Christ-like mind that honors Him. Let's love Him with our minds!

Jesus replied: "Love the Lord your God with all your heart and with all your soul and with all your mind." (Matthew 22:37)

Set your minds on things above, not on earthly things. (Colossians 3:2)

You will keep in perfect peace him whose mind is steadfast, because he trusts in you. (Isaiah 26:3)

The salvation of the righteous comes from the LORD; he is their stronghold in time of trouble. (Psalm 37:39)

The helmet of salvation serves to remind us that nothing can snatch us out of God's hand. Our salvation does not come and go based on success and failure in our lives. From experience, when we make a royal mess of things and fall into sin, Satan will pounce on this opportunity to suggest we can't possibly be saved, thus having us doubt our salvation. We have to remember that eternal life is based on fact, not feeling. His craftiness can also be seen when we are struggling with a weakness, affliction or hit with oppression. Remember, he is the father of lies. Praise God that we can walk in total security when we are dressed in His armor.

This helmet also reminds us that the Lord is our salvation:

He put on righteousness as his breastplate, and the helmet of salvation on his head... (Isaiah 59:17)

The LORD is my light and my salvation – whom shall I fear? The LORD is the stronghold of my life of whom shall I be afraid? (Psalm 27:1)

O sovereign LORD, my strong deliverer, who shields my head in the day of battle. (Psalm 140:7)

For the LORD takes delight in his people; he crowns the humble with salvation. (Psalm 149:4)

Finally, we take into our hand the sharp, double-edged sword.

The Sword of the Spirit

The sword of the spirit is the Word of God. The sword is the only weapon of offense in these pieces listed; therefore it is very important to learn all we can about the Word of God.

The Bible is your most powerful weapon in defeating the devil. Remember earlier when we established that the truth was the most powerful weapon? God's Word *is* truth. That's one of the reasons it is so important to spend time reading and memorizing God's words to us. It sharpens our sword. Dear friends, I pray that the more you feed yourself with the words of God that you also will taste and see that the Lord is good. (Psalm 34:8)

Reading, speaking and clinging to scripture became an important key to surviving the heated battle. Many nights, weary from pain and weakness, I did not have strength to read the pages that had become so precious to me, so I would lie in bed with my Bible tucked into my side. Somehow, it was a comfort to me when everything around me seemed to be falling apart. Jesus was my firm foundation.

I believe that the Word has preserved my life as stated in Psalm 119. This psalm also tells us to hide God's Word in our hearts so we will not sin against Him. Hiding scripture in our hearts is extremely effective and over time you will build up an arsenal. Hebrews 4:12 gives us a remarkable description of our sword: *"For the word of God is living and active. Sharper than any double-edged sword, it penetrates even to dividing soul and spirit, joints and marrow; it judges the thoughts and attitudes of the heart."* That's an amazing sword!

Another light bulb moment occurred as I realized this sword of the Spirit is the very same weapon that the Holy Spirit uses! The Holy Spirit uses the Word to convict our hearts, to instruct and teach, to encourage, lead and tenderly comfort us. The Spirit also uses the Word to fight for us in the heavenly realms.

If you have received Jesus Christ as your Savior then the Holy Spirit dwells in you. Over time, as you memorize and meditate on scripture, your declaration of scripture will be powerful to demolish strongholds (2 Corinthians 10:4). This practice has changed my life.

When temptation comes your way or fear grips your heart, respond immediately by speaking a verse out loud if you can. It is amazing to me how the Holy Spirit can quicken within us a verse of scripture at the precise moment of need. Sometimes it may be a verse that we haven't heard in years. Speaking the Word will give you strength to stand and resist the devil. This is one of the ways we use this awesome weapon. I love this beautiful scripture:

The Sovereign LORD has given me an instructed tongue, to know the word that sustains the weary. He

*wakens me morning by morning, wakens my ear to
listen like one being taught.* (Isaiah 50:4)

The Lord will also give us a verse of scripture or a word
of encouragement to lift up others. These timely words can be
a tremendous blessing to the one receiving *and* to the one
giving. I have often received encouragement in this way and it
has given me hope and strength to go on. (If it hadn't been for
an encouraging word from a friend, I would have never
written this particular chapter). On the other hand: *"Reckless
words pierce like a sword, but the tongue of the wise brings
healing"* (Proverbs 12:18).

Our tongues can either cut like daggers or deliver
precious words of life. "Speak words of life," as my pastor
says. Taking up the sword reminds me to pray for my tongue.
Because I don't always speak kindly to my husband, I had to
memorize, *"Set a guard over my mouth, O LORD; keep watch
over the door of my lips"* (Psalm 141:3). The tongue is a tough
muscle to tame, but with God's help nothing is impossible.
Cover it in prayer and hit it with the sword! I was surprised to
find over 300 references to the word "mouth" in the Bible
such as this: *"...For out of the overflow of the heart the mouth
speaks"* (Matthew 12:34).

The great English preacher, C.H. Spurgeon, wrote this
about the Christian warrior:

To be a Christian is to be a warrior. The good soldier
of Jesus Christ must not expect to find ease in this
world: it is a battlefield. Neither must he reckon upon
the friendship of the world; for that would be enmity
against God. His occupation is war. As he puts on
piece by piece the panoply provided for him, he may

wisely say to himself, "This warns me of danger, this prepares me for warfare, this prophesies opposition." He goes on to say, "Difficulties meet us even in standing our ground; for the apostle, two or three times, bids us— Stand.[5]

In the book of Matthew, chapter four, Jesus himself had to stand three times when he was tempted in the desert. After he had fasted forty days and nights the devil came to Him, and since Jesus was hungry Satan told him to turn the stones into bread.

Jesus answered, "It is written; 'Man does not live on bread alone, but on every word that comes from the mouth of God.'" (Matthew 4:4)

Then the devil took him to the highest point in the city and tempting him again said, "If you are the Son of God, throw yourself down" (vs. 5). Then Satan quoted Psalm 91, out of context:

For it is written: "He will command his angels concerning you, and they will lift you up in their hands, so that you will not strike your foot against a stone." (vs.6) Jesus answered him, "It is also written: 'Do not put the Lord your God to the test'" (vs. 7).

Our enemy does not give up easily, because he again took Jesus to a high mountain and tempted him a third time. He showed him all the kingdoms of the world (vs.8).

"All this I will give you," he said, "if you will bow down and worship me." Jesus said to him, "Away from me, Satan! For it is written: 'Worship the Lord your God, and serve him only.'" Then the devil left him, and angels came and attended him (vs. 9-11).

This account from Matthew shows how important and effective it is to know and apply the Word of God to combat temptation. We must take up the sword!

Friends, we should ask the Holy Spirit to teach us how to wield this mysterious, powerful, spiritual weapon. It may take time to learn this, but we have a wise and patient teacher. Scripture goes on to describe more about the sword of the Spirit:

Do not let this Book of the Law depart from your mouth; meditate on it day and night, so that you may be careful to do everything written in it. Then you will be prosperous and successful. (Joshua 1:8)

I have hidden your word in my heart that I might not sin against you. (Psalm 119:11)

May the praise of God be in their mouths and a double-edged sword in their hands. (Psalm 149:6)

In that day, the LORD will punish with his sword, his fierce, great and powerful sword... (Isaiah 27:1)

He made my mouth like a sharpened sword, in the shadow of his hand he hid me; he made me into a

polished arrow and concealed me in his quiver.
(Isaiah 49:2)

In his right hand he held seven stars, and out of his mouth came a sharp double-edged sword.
(Revelation 1:16)

...These are the words of him who has the sharp, double-edged sword. (Revelation 2:12)

I cannot close without reiterating the importance of prayer. It has impacted my life in such a profound way. I could write a book on what God has done in my life just through prayer alone! Had it not been for the faithful prayers of believers I wouldn't be alive today. What an awesome privilege it is to talk and listen to the One who formed the universe.

Prayer is a divine weapon that we don't use nearly enough. I believe if we knew how effective our prayers are in fighting battles in the heavenly realms we would be astounded. For me this is a hard discipline— one that I am diligently working on. My desire has always been to wake at 5:00 a.m. and pray. Well, I can count on two hands in forty years when that has happened. I hate to admit it, but I envy those who wake up before the chickens. Proverbs 31 haunts me where it talks about the woman who gets up while it is still dark. Personally, I seem to be able to concentrate in prayer more effectively on the night shift...at least it is dark then! Regardless of *when* we pray, we should pray in the Spirit on all occasions with all kinds of prayers and requests (Ephesians 6:18).

John Wesley says this about prayer: *"God does nothing but in answer to prayer."*[6]

Bible teacher and author Beth Moore states: *"Prayerless lives are powerless lives."*[7]

What the Bible says about prayer:

Call to me and I will answer you and tell you great and unsearchable things that you do not know. (Jeremiah 33:3)

If you abide in Me, and My words abide in you, ask whatever you wish, and it will be done for you. (John 15:7 NASB)

Be joyful in hope, patient in affliction, faithful in prayer. (Romans 12:12)

Rejoice always; pray without ceasing; in everything give thanks; for this is God's will for you in Christ Jesus. (1 Thessalonians 5:16-18 NASB)

I know that this has been a long chapter. Thank you for persevering! Please stay with me a moment longer, as I briefly share something weighing heavily on me regarding prayer, and what we must do in this fight against the evil forces in our world.

I looked for a man among them who would build up a wall and stand in the gap on behalf of the land so I would not have to destroy it, but I found none. (Ezekiel 22:30)

When I read this verse two years ago, it grieved me so much that I wept. I am reminded of the shields that were linked together to build up a line of defense so the soldiers could move forward against the enemy, achieving victory.

As believers, we need to repent, get on our knees and build up a strong wall of prayer so God will not destroy our land. I know many of you are praying. May Jesus find not one, but tens of thousands standing in the gap praying fervently for our land. As I close this chapter would you join me in praying 2 Chronicles 14:11 over our nation?

LORD, there is no one like you to help the powerless against the mighty. Help us O LORD our God, for we rely on you, and in your name we have come against this vast army. O LORD, you are our God; do not let man prevail against you.

My heartfelt prayer is that these pages have blessed your life in a powerful way, leaving you forever changed.

The LORD is with you, mighty warrior. (Judges 6:12)

What I Learned Lying Down

Chapter 15

Judged by the Court

The friend who can be silent with us in a moment of despair or confusion, who can stay with us in an hour of grief and bereavement, who can tolerate not knowing, not curing, not healing and face with us the reality of our powerlessness, that is a friend who cares. --- Henri Nouwen[8]

Just a few weeks before I was to send this to the publisher, the Lord reminded me that the book was not finished. My talks with the Lord went something like this: "Lord, are you sure that this chapter is really necessary? I already touched on the subject earlier, isn't that enough?" You see, one reason I hesitated in writing on this topic is because just as I have been unfairly judged, I too, have sat as judge.

The Lord nudged me to include this chapter after an awful doctor appointment. For almost thirty minutes, my frustrated doctor sat as judge and jury, while I sat with a fever and pain, trying to defend myself.

He swung the gavel hard, pronouncing his judgment on my outlook and even my faith. But what stung the most was his statement that I was not victorious, and that I could not glorify God if I was lying sick in bed or in pain! His statements were like a strong punch in the gut. How unprepared I was for this confrontation. But remember, that is exactly how those fiery darts come—without warning.

That morning I could barely get out of bed and had not yet put on my armor, my daughter was home sick with the flu, I was on pain pills for pleurisy, and was not in any way ready to be put on the stand. Something I forgot during the appointment was that the Lord is our defender. Yes, He is the only one qualified to judge. *"For the LORD is our judge, the Lord is our lawgiver..."* (Isaiah 33:22).

Most of my life I have run from confrontation as fast as my short legs could carry me. I have prayed to be more assertive and have sought counsel to help me deal with confrontation. Last week, I finally stopped running. It was the same doctor appointment and I was again being questioned and "put down" because my body wasn't responding like it should. Progress was made though; I spoke the truth in love, a doormat no longer! In hindsight, I can now see that the Lord has brought me one test after another to teach me to deal with conflict.

Why do some doctors sit as judge over their patients? Why must we fit into their box or be labeled? We are not objects; rather each of us is an individual – fearfully and wonderfully made. I do understand that diseases like lupus are unpredictable, and frustrating to diagnose and treat, but why is it that when the patient does not fit the mold, suddenly *they* are the problem?

If you suffer with illness that is chronic, some people find it hard to stand by and give support without eventually starting to question your emotions, your attitude or your faith. Sometimes friends or family just walk away. Unfortunately, this rejection is all too common, leaving the afflicted one feeling unimportant, alone and devastated. There is no doubt that it takes a special person to be a faithful friend to the chronically ill.

Thankfully, I've been blessed with some loyal friends and family members, but unfortunately I've had so many more who became my critics. Others would want my friendship when I was having good days, but as soon as I had a flare they would stay away or not call.

Many unjust judges have tried my case—doctors, church members, friends and even close family members. Criticism often hurts more than the pain of disease. And then there were those who brought subtle things like books and videos that suggested sin or lack of faith was the reason I was not healed.

Words of judgment cut deep, right to the heart. Why do the healthy sometimes judge the sick? We want to be understood, not placed under a microscope. Unfortunately, some cannot grasp the word "chronic," so they begin to speculate why you are not getting better. I know a beautiful Christian lady that battles depression and she has said to me, "Why do Christians shoot their wounded?" I wish I knew the answer.

I believe we can learn much from the story about the blind man in the gospel of John 9:1-3. *As he* (Jesus) *went along, he saw a man blind from birth. His disciples asked him, "Rabbi, who sinned, this man or his parents, that he was born blind?" "Neither this man nor his parents sinned," said Jesus, "but this happened so that the work of God might be displayed in his life."*

The Father has given Jesus the authority to judge, and Jesus gives many stern warnings on the subject. In fact, after I studied the scriptures included on these pages, I was on my knees. Jesus spoke in his famous Sermon on the Mount:

Why do you look at the speck of sawdust in your brother's eye and pay no attention to the plank in your own eye? How can you say to your brother, 'Let me take the speck out of your eye,' when all the time there is a plank in your own eye? You hypocrite, first take the plank out of your eye, and then you can see clearly to remove the speck out of your brother's eye. (Matthew 7:3-5)

Why do we cast stones? My medical case obviously did not fit the "formula." I think most of us want life to make sense, such as $1+1 = 2$, but my situation was more like $A + E = Z-3$. When I did not fit the medical "math", the solution was to judge me as the problem. Of course we don't throw rocks; we throw words—like gossip, criticism and rash judgments, and they can wound severely.

Perhaps we would rather judge others than look at what the Lord is trying to show us about our own hearts. We speculate when we don't have all the facts. "*Stop judging by mere appearances and make a right judgment*" (John 7:24). Jesus knows our thoughts as well, and His judgment is based on truth. He alone knows all the facts.

Please understand, I am not saying that we are to walk around ignoring false teaching or sinful behavior. Not *all* judgment is wrong if it is based on scripture. Jesus clearly tells us to make a *right* judgment, and the Bible clearly instructs us so we can make that right judgment against sin. For example, we can make right judgments against things like sexual immorality, open sin in the church or rebellion against authority; however, we are to do this in love.

If you have someone in your life that is battling health issues, ask the Lord to give you patience and empathy, even when there seems to be no comprehending the situation. If there is obvious sin or even self-defeating behavior, then pray that you may deliver the message in gentleness and love.

To those who know the pain of rejection and being misunderstood, I may have a few words of insight for you. Many times, I think we expect too much from friends, family and onlookers. They can support us, and we desperately need that, but ultimately we endure it alone. During instances where I was misunderstood or rejected, I felt the Lord was teaching me that *He* is the only one who can fully understand the weight of the cross I bear. Jesus was left alone when His friends were needed the most, in the garden of Gethsemane the night before His crucifixion. He needed His friends *desperately* at that moment, and they had fallen asleep. (Matthew 26:40)

In this life we will be rejected, misunderstood, persecuted, judged unfairly and left alone. We are taking part in the sufferings of Christ when we endure adversity. When I don't understand – I go to the Word. This week I stumbled upon this verse, *"For it has been granted to you on behalf of Christ not only to believe on him, but also to suffer for him..."* (Philippians 1:29).

So perhaps we should realize that whether we are sick or well, we will suffer trials and tribulation. If we see someone going through a difficult test we should be careful to empathize, encourage and offer support, but slow to judge and criticize. We must know that God often uses these trials to accomplish His purposes, bringing glory to His name.

What I Learned Lying Down

Chapter 16

Homesick

...No eye has seen, no ear has heard, no mind has conceived what God has prepared for those who love him, but God has revealed it to us by his Spirit.
(1 Corinthians 2:9 & 10)

Some might say of me that I'm so heavenly minded that I'm no earthly good. However, my father-in-law, whom I love dearly, once said that we can't be any earthly good, *unless* we're heavenly minded. To make the most impact for Christ, we want to be kingdom-focused people, seeking first His kingdom and His righteousness, and then all other things will be given to us as well (Matthew 6:33).

Ever since I can remember, I've always been fascinated about this magnificent and mysterious place called Heaven. As a little girl I had dreams of heaven, solidifying this beautiful place in my heart and mind. Yet I continue to be amazed that the God of the universe would prepare a place for us not made with human hands. I can't help but think, "Lord, we are so unworthy, that you would build a home for us?" But in the book of John, that is exactly what Jesus tells us.

Do not let your hearts be troubled. Trust in God; trust also in me. In my Father's house are many rooms; if it were not so, I would have told you. I am going there to prepare a place for you. And if I go to prepare a place for you, I will come back and take you to be with me that you may also be where I am. (John 14:1-3)

Heaven is my real home! How could I love a home so much that I have never seen? Because my Savior is there! I'm eagerly waiting for that blessed hope and the glorious appearing of our Savior Jesus Christ (Titus 2:13). Another reason is that my heart and mind have been turned upward as a result of this sick body. I yearn to be clothed with my heavenly dwelling and fall before the Lord's feet. I can hardly wait for the "Sonlight" that won't make me sick, shiny long hair that won't fall out, strong legs that will run and jump, as well as a smile that won't fade from pain.

I will forever be free from physicians, pain and pills! Don't mistake me, I do pray that my doctors will be there, but praise God they will have a new occupation. I find myself wishing that I could hang up this tent that I have been given on earth and be free. I dream of heaven for there I will be healed.

Many times, I have felt torn in two like the apostle Paul describes—as if I had one foot down on earth and the other one firmly planted in heaven. I wanted to go and be with the Lord on one hand, but remain here for my husband and children on the other. As believers we long for a time when the battle will cease and the sin that so easily entangles us will be no more.

Dear ones, Christ will soon return, and we must prepare the way for the Lord. But how easily we forget this and are caught up in the trappings of this world.

It is clear to me, from talking with others that the distractions of our hectic lifestyles keep us from being about our Father's business. Busyness is one of Satan's clever tools and he uses it skillfully. He uses even "good things" to sidetrack us from "best things" God has for us.

At the time of this writing Christmas is a week away and I can easily see how stressed people are with the madness of the holiday. I want to celebrate Jesus, but each December I can't wait until January so the craziness of it all will be over!

Christmas isn't about Christ anymore. There are lists to be made, stockings to fill, shopping, school programs and cookies to bake. Parties to plan, presents to wrap, lights to be hung and cards to be sent. The tree must be trimmed and ornaments hung, decorating done and songs to be sung. No wonder my body crashes every December (and I can only do the minimum)! It seems insane.

Don't you know that it must grieve God when His children are so attracted to this world, not looking for His return? We are so focused on worldly treasures that little attention is given to the treasures that we are to store in eternity. Jesus said:

> *Do not store up for yourselves treasures on earth, where moth and rust destroy, and where thieves break in and steal. But store up for yourselves treasures in heaven, where moth and rust do not destroy, and where thieves do not break in and steal. For where your treasure is, there your heart will be also.* (Matthew 6:19-21).

Temporary possessions here cannot begin to compare with eternal, everlasting riches there! Perhaps some of us would say that material things have a grip on us, but don't you agree we should be in His grip instead? Perhaps the closer we grow in our relationship with Christ, the more homesick we become. When you get a taste of that sweet fellowship with the Lord, it leaves you craving for more. I desire it more than anything else on earth.

Our human minds cannot comprehend the inexpressible and glorious joy that will be experienced when we are finally home. When we all are united worshipping our Savior, it's going to be indescribable. No longer will we feel like aliens in a foreign land, but we will be in that place that our Spirit has longed to be. In 2 Corinthians chapter 5 we are told that the Holy Spirit is a deposit or down payment of what is to come (vs.5). I can relate strongly with the groaning and longing to be clothed with our heavenly dwelling as described below:

> *Now we know that if the earthly tent we live in is destroyed, we have a building from God, an eternal house in heaven, not built by human hands. Meanwhile we groan, longing to be clothed with our heavenly dwelling, because when we are clothed, we will not be found naked. For while in this tent, we groan and are burdened, because we do not wish to be unclothed but to be clothed with our heavenly dwelling, so that what is mortal may be swallowed up by life. Now it is God who has made us for this very purpose and has given us the Spirit as a deposit, guaranteeing what is to come. (2 Corinthians 5:1-5)*

For those who have received Christ as Savior, the eternal bliss to come surpasses what our earthly minds can even remotely take hold of. One night, God gave me a glimpse of heaven in a beautiful dream, one that I will cherish in my heart always. The dream came at a time when my marriage was struggling to survive. I was physically weakened from pain, emotionally distressed and deeply in need of comfort from many rounds of spiritual warfare. I believe these are some of the reasons that the dream was given to me.

Just reflecting upon it has brought comfort through the pain. I thank my heavenly Father for giving me this beautiful gift. My sincere hope is that by sharing this, it might encourage those of you who are weary. I'll forever carry this with me until my work on earth is done, and I go home to explore all the wonders of this place we call heaven.

August 13, 2007

What a glorious dream! I arrived by boat to a place that I did not recognize. There was a curved channel of water leading up to a place so magnificent, I can hardly describe it. The boat ride was so quiet that I heard no motor. And as it came to a gentle stop, I stepped out on a marble landing that led me through a gorgeous courtyard. As I stood in front of this massive structure I remember thinking, "Who would have invited me to this grand palace?" As the boat moved on, I stared at the glistening rocks along this river bed and the gorgeous vines and plants. The water was so clear that I was able to see massive rocks on the bottom and on the sides of the waterway. Curious as to why these rocks were so striking, I leaned forward to get a closer look and a voice behind me said, *"The rocks that you are looking at are gemstones."* Those were the only words that were spoken to me the entire time. I looked behind me but no one was there. As I walked through the courtyard, I looked around at all the beautiful lattice work and then like a curious child, I eagerly walked up the white marble steps.

Opening the massive doors, I was mesmerized with what surrounded me. My senses were overloaded with sweet aromas, extraordinary sights and the most beautiful sounds.

I was stunned by the architecture of this place. The colors that caught my eye were not that of beautiful flowers like you would expect, but of gems built into the marble columns. There were even chairs and benches made out of these stones. Luminous emeralds, rubies, garnets, sapphires and other brilliant gems were built into the walls and pearly white columns. What was even more impressive was that this appeared to be an enclosed city. As I looked up, I saw beautiful crystal tiles that were transparent like glass which served as a ceiling. It felt as if I was outside, and inside at the same time.

The trees were strong and gorgeous with the leaves swaying as if a gentle wind was blowing. I slowly walked along a path outlined in the greenest grass my eyes have ever seen. It was so lush that I did not even want to step on it. There were people bustling around this enclosed city, but what intrigued me now was what I was hearing— the most melodic music —and I was determined to find out where it was coming from.

As I walked along the path, I heard clanking in the background that interrupted the beautiful heavenly music. "What is that noise? It just does not fit the peaceful surroundings," I thought.

Unfortunately, what I was hearing was my daughter unloading the dishwasher in the kitchen. She was doing her chores without being asked and any other day I would have been overjoyed. My first waking thought was, "No, I want to go back to that place!" So, closing my eyes I reflected on… "heavenly music…giant gems…walking along the path…*please* go back to sleep." But it was no use.

Lying in bed that morning, I knew this was no ordinary dream. My first inclination was that I had possibly seen a glimpse of the New Jerusalem. One day, I will recognize with my own eyes what the Lord so graciously allowed me to see.

It has been over two years now since my dream of heaven, and I can still see it clearly in my mind. Without a doubt, I know it was sent from God for reasons known only to Him. One may be so that I could share it with those who are in desperate need of hope, above and beyond what this world can offer.

When we meet Jesus face to face, I don't believe we will have any questions to ask. In this dream I asked nothing, and remained in a state of absolute awe. Perhaps when we see our Savior, any questions we have will be answered in our Spirit instantly. One thing is certain, I want to be ready to meet Jesus when He comes to take me home. The finish line is in sight and He *is* coming soon! Are you ready?

For here we do not have an enduring city, but we are looking for the city that is to come. (Hebrews 13:14)

What I Learned Lying Down

Chapter 17

Be Encouraged

Therefore encourage one another and build each other up... (1 Thessalonians 5:11)

We live in a society where you are what you can accomplish; people are running to and fro while the weak, elderly and sick are left behind. Sadly, some are completely forgotten. The afflicted cannot survive the hurried pace and quite frankly, sometimes all we can do is "be." What then is our purpose with a body that holds us captive? How are we to cope in this world that spins faster and faster while we function at a crawl?

While watching television one night a few years ago, I heard a story about a man who was a quadriplegic. The statement that shook me from self-pity was when he said with confidence, "I am *not* my body." My eyes filled with tears as I pondered his profound statement. We are so much more than what our bodies can accomplish; we are survivors! We have a brain, a soul, a personality and we have hopes, dreams and talents like anyone else.

In addition, we each have a role in life regardless of our physical state; we continue to have a "position" designated by God. It may be that you are a son or daughter, brother, sister, father, mother, grandparent or friend. When my confinement and disabilities depressed me to the point of feeling useless, my husband would constantly remind me, "Regardless of how sick you are, no matter what you cannot do, you are the *only* one who can be Mom. No one can replace you!"

My friend, *you are valuable* in a wheelchair, in a hospital bed, on your sick bed and yes, even on your death bed! In fact, Jesus says we are of much value to him: *"Look at the birds of the air; they do not sow or reap or store away in barns, and yet your heavenly Father feeds them. Are you not much more valuable than they?" (Matthew 6:26).* No one is insignificant or worthless, from the tiny unborn, to the one who is about to take his last breath, you are a pearl of great price (Matthew 13:45-46)!

There are many things you can still contribute to this world. You can encourage others, you can teach and you can love. As I have mentioned before, I strongly believe that the Lord sets some aside for prayer. Prayer is absolutely critical in our world today, especially given the evil days we live in. We may not be marathon runners, but we can be mountain movers!

Don't ever forget that God has a unique plan and a purpose for you (Jeremiah 29:11). Just because you are homebound, bedridden or living with chronic pain doesn't mean for a single second that you cannot fulfill the purpose that God has for you. Even if you feel like a weight holding down the couch, like I did, you still have a divine purpose. As my Mississippi mama would say, "God don't make no junk."

The Bible tells us that God chooses the weak things of this world to shame the strong (1 Corinthians 1:27). In the book of Romans it states so beautifully, *"...but we also rejoice in our sufferings, because we know that suffering produces perseverance; perseverance character; and character hope. And hope does not disappoint us, because God has poured out his love into our hearts by the Holy Spirit, whom he has given us."* (Romans 5:3-5)

If you have suffered through trials for very long, you already know what it means to persevere. This passage in Romans tells us that we have gained perseverance, character and hope through suffering. Our bodies are simply jars of clay that carry us around, but inside we have a spirit, a voice, gifts and life lessons to share. We are the temple of God!

But we have this treasure in jars of clay to show that this all- surpassing power is from God and not from us. We are hard pressed on every side, but not crushed; perplexed, but not in despair; persecuted, but not abandoned; struck down, but not destroyed. (2 Corinthians 4:7-9)

The Holy Spirit is the treasure that fills us with power and strength to persevere. His strength is exactly what is needed as we, like salmon, swim upstream. It is a constant uphill climb for those of us who face a life-threatening disease, and it is so important to know that when we can't – He can!

He gives strength to the weary and increases the power of the weak. Even youths grow tired and weary, and young men stumble and fall; but those who hope in the LORD will renew their strength. They will soar on wings like eagles; they will run and not grow weary, they will walk and not be faint. (Isaiah 40:29-31)

Once, while my blood was being drawn for the umpteenth time, a sweet lab technician encouraged me to read Psalm

40:1-3. It just so happened that I had a Bible in our car, so I was able to be refreshed by this beautiful verse just minutes later. It was like water to my soul and remains one of my favorites. Remember, the Lord acts on behalf of those who wait for Him (Isaiah 64:4), so hang on to these verses knowing that one day your trial will end.

I waited patiently for the LORD; he turned to me and heard my cry. He lifted me out of the slimy pit, out of the mud and mire; he set my feet on a rock and gave me a firm place to stand. He put a new song in my mouth, a hymn of praise to our God. Many will see and fear and put their trust in the LORD. (Psalm 40:1-3)

The Lord has put a new song in my mouth, and He will do the same for you! So, let us hold unswervingly to the hope we profess, because He who promised is faithful. (Hebrews 10:23)

My heart wishes I could hug each one of you who are sick and lonely, left behind, shut-in, cancer-stricken, and those with a mysterious illness. I understand those who have no answers yet suffer in silence. Whatever the circumstances that led you to pick up this book; I believe that it was no mistake. Perhaps you don't battle a chronic illness, but are in the heat of another battle, or maybe you are the exhausted caregiver. Whatever the case may be, Jesus loves you, and He says to His followers today, *"...Never will I leave you; never will I forsake you"* (Hebrews 13:5).

If you don't know this Jesus that I have been writing about, you can know Him today. As you have read my story, it is my heart's desire that you have been drawn to our Savior and friend - Jesus. The one who has been my ever-present

Help in times of trouble, the Faithful One, the Great "I AM", the Redeemer and Healer, Comforter, Sustainer and my Everything.

Maybe you know about Jesus, but don't *know* Him. Dear friend, if that is you, and you want to know the peace and hope that is only found in Christ, don't delay. *"For God so loved the world that he gave his one and only Son, that whoever believes in him shall not perish but have eternal life"* (John 3:16). He is the **only** way you can be saved and enter into heaven.

Salvation is found in no one else, for there is no other name under heaven given to men by which we must be saved. (Acts 4:12)

You see, all have sinned and fall short of the glory of God (Romans 3:23), but if we confess our sins He is faithful and just to forgive our sins and cleanse us of all unrighteousness (1 John 1:9). None of us are perfect. We have all broken God's laws and the payment for our sin is death (Romans 6:23).

But God demonstrates his own love toward us in this: While we were still sinners, Christ died for us. (Romans 5:8)

That is the good news! Jesus made a way for us to be reconciled to the Father through His precious shed blood on the cross.

For it is by grace you have been saved, through faith—and this not from yourselves, it is the gift of

God—not by works, so that no one can boast.
(Ephesians 2:8-9)

We are saved by God's undeserved favor called grace. It is a free gift! Your religion cannot get you into heaven. Volunteering at the church won't do it either. But you are a good person and you help feed the poor (sorry, that falls under "works"). Trusting in your Savior and Him alone is the only way you can receive this beautiful free gift of salvation.

Everyone who calls on the name of the Lord will be saved. (Romans 10:13)

This verse does not mean that God will heal you of physical illness, although He can; but that your soul will be saved! Our soul is the part of us that never dies. After our bodies die, our souls live on forever in either heaven or hell. I plead with you to choose Jesus and Heaven before it is too late! Only a personal relationship with Jesus Christ can satisfy the deepest longings of our hearts, regardless of what our physical condition may be. The door is open now and the Lord is patiently waiting, however one day the door will close forever.

...I tell you, now is the time of God's favor, now is the day of salvation. (2 Corinthians 6:2)

Would you like to trust Jesus Christ as your Savior? If you answered yes, why not talk to Him now. It might sound something like this:

"Dear Lord, I know that I'm a sinner. I am tired of running my own life. I want to turn away from my way of doing things, to living God's way. I repent of my sins and ask you to forgive me. Wash my heart clean and rescue me. I surrender to you Jesus and trust you alone as my Savior. I believe Christ died for me and rose from the grave. I confess Jesus as Lord of my life. From this moment on, help me to follow you all the days of my life. In Your name, Amen."

Here I am! I stand at the door and knock. If anyone hears my voice and opens the door, I will come in and eat with him, and he with me. (Revelation 3:20)

To find out more about following Christ, visit:
www.ichristianlife.com

What I Learned Lying Down

In Closing

When I knew without a doubt that God was calling me to do more than just journal, I said, "Lord, I know nothing about writing a book, and I think you're asking me to do the impossible." The thought itself overwhelmed me.

But this has always been about Him. Now I hold the "impossible" in my lap. It seems kind of ironic that one of my favorite verses is Matthew 19:26, *"With man this is impossible but with God all things are possible."* I knew the truth of this verse, but my circumstances paralyzed me.

I was wading through thick spiritual warfare (doubt, depression, condemnation and confusion), painful flare-ups, fainting spells and lots of days in bed. There were doctor visits, procedures and medications all while raising three kids and trying to be a godly wife. So it was hard to imagine and even *outrageous* to think that this project could be accomplished.

I hope my story will encourage someone to trust God in impossible circumstances. Perhaps you are staring at your Goliath instead of your God, like I was. Remember:

Now to him who is able to do immeasurably more than all we ask or imagine, according to his power that is at work within us, to him be glory in the church and in Christ Jesus throughout all generations, forever and ever! Amen
(Ephesians 3:20-21).

As this manuscript goes to print, I can hardly believe what God has written through this weak vessel. I thank God for the joy and strength He has given to me in writing this for His glory. He is forever faithful to complete that which He has begun in us (Philippians 1:6)!

Even though the physical battle goes on; I am blessed and content. I have accepted that this trial is by God's design and not a mistake. *"As for God, His way is perfect..."* (Psalm 18:30) God has not changed my condition, but He has changed me. My prayers have changed as well. While I still hope for healing, I no longer plead with God. Instead, I pray that whatever trials I must walk through that they will bear fruit for the kingdom. My desire is for Christ to be exalted in my body (Phil. 1:20). May Jesus alone receive all the praise, honor and glory that is due Him!

End Notes

1. George MacDonald. Public Domain

2. From the book, *Mountain Breezes: The Collected Poems of Amy Carmichael*, Copyright 1999 by the Dohnavur Fellowship, and published by CLC Publications, Fort Washington, PA. Used by permission. All rights reserved.

3. Jean Paul Richter. Public Domain.

4. Warren Wiersbe. *What to Wear to the War.* Copyright 1986 by Back to the Bible Publishing. Used by permission.

5. C.H. Spurgeon. Public Domain

6. John Wesley. Public Domain

7. Beth Moore. *Praying God's Word.* Copyright 2000, 2003 by Broadman & Holman Publishers. Reprinted and used by permission.

8. Henri J. M. Nouwen. *Out of Solitude.* Copyright 1974, 2004 by Ave Maria Press, Inc., P.O. Box 428, Notre Dame, IN 46556. Used with permission of the publisher.

For more information contact:

Angela Dugi
C/O Advantage Books
P.O. Box 160847
Altamonte Springs, Florida 32716

To purchase additional copies of this book or other books published
by Advantage Books call our toll free order number at:
1-888-383-3110 (Book Orders Only)

or visit our bookstore website at:
www.advbookstore.com

Longwood, Florida, USA
"we bring dreams to life"™
www.advbooks.com

LaVergne, TN USA
30 October 2010
202785LV00003B/10/P